THREADS
of HONOR

The True Story of a Boy Scout Troop,
Perseverance, Triumph, and
an American Flag

Revised and Expanded Second Edition

BY GORDON RYAN

foreword by U.S. Senator Orrin Hatch

Mapletree Publishing Company

Published by Mapletree Publishing Company
Denver, Colorado
800-537-0414
e-mail: mail@mapletreepublishing.com
www.mapletreepublishing.com

Cover design by George Foster, www.fostercovers.com

Second edition
Previous edition copyright © 1996 by Gordon W. Ryan and
published by Deseret Book Company, Salt Lake City, Utah

Library of Congress Cataloging-in-Publication Data
Ryan, Gordon,
Threads of honor : the true story of a Boy Scout troop, perseverance,
triumph, and an American flag / by Gordon Ryan ; foreword by Orrin
Hatch.—Rev. and expanded 2nd ed.
p. cm.
Includes index.
ISBN 0-9728071-0-1
1. Flags—United States. 2. Boy Scouts—Colorado 3. Challenger
(Spacecraft)—Accidents. I. Title.
CR113.B927 2003
929.9'2—dc22   2003014832

The Mapletree logo is a trademark of Mapletree Publishing Company

Printed in the United States of America

TABLE OF CONTENTS

For my three scouting sons:
Tom, who has gone on ahead;
Mike, who brings us great joy; and
Danny, who has been endowed with the potential to
surpass us all,
with all my love.

and dedicated to my two lifelong friends,

Judge George G. Granata, whose personal example during
our formative high school years provided for me the
incentive to seek a better way, and whose premature
death after twenty years as a distinguished jurist has left
a void in my life.

and

William A. Tolbert, who, through his friendship, afforded
me the opportunity to share that better way, and who, for
nearly forty years, has continued to provide his personal
example of persistence, honor, and integrity, as well as
his brotherly love.

And to Scoutmasters everywhere.
Would that all had such friends.

FOREWORD

The American flag is more than just a piece of cloth — it symbolizes the courage of many, and the hope of our nation. From the frontiers of America's earliest days to today's battlefields — the American flag has always represented courage, hope and perseverance. *Threads of Honor* is about one particular American flag whose threads touched the lives of many and whose journey inspired our nation. In today's troubled times when America is being bombarded by those who try to threaten our democracy and the freedoms we hold dear, this book will give readers a stirring reminder of the many men and women who have sacrificed, and in some instances given everything, for what the flag represents — our freedom.

Threads of Honor is a wonderful portrait of a Boy Scout troop that wouldn't give up, their leader who instills loyalty and steadfastness, and an American flag that changed their lives forever. It is about America's space program and the frontiers it conquers. And it is a story of a journey that a small group of young men and one American flag took to help comfort a grieving nation. In short, *Threads of Honor* is an inspiring portrayal of the triumph of the human spirit.

U.S. Senator Orrin G. Hatch

A thoughtful mind
when it sees a nation's flag,
sees not the flag, but the nation itself.
—Henry Ward Beecher

PREFACE

Threads of Honor relates a true story about a Boy Scout troop and an American flag. However, the dialogue in this account did not happen exactly as written, and some of the minor characters are not real. The significant characters, however, are all real. Bill Tolbert was asked to be the scoutmaster of Boy Scout Troop 514 in Monument, Colorado, as the story indicates. The flag they obtained for their troop was indeed a Valley Forge flag that had flown over the United States Capitol. The other events detailed in this account, as amazing as they seem, all happened.

This book is about a basic human need and one of God's greatest gifts: human liberty, or moral agency, each of which provides us the right to choose to do good or to do evil.

Though it is a gift from God, the freedom to choose is not easily retained. Through the ages devious and selfish men — the tyrants of history and even those of the present day — have sought control over others, and wars have been fought to determine whether or not freedom will endure.

I firmly believe that human beings can reach their full potential only in a society that provides freedom of choice. Restrictions of our ability to choose confine the soul, stifle our ability to learn (or even to dream), limit our creativity and ambition, and stunt our intellectual and spiritual growth. The commitment we have to others' right to choose is a measure of the respect we have for people as individuals, and is therefore an indicator of the depth of our own character.

I came of age in the sixties — an eclectic era when people were confronted with many moral choices. Some of the choices made by people my age were not sound, but the mere fact that we *had* choices made it a glorious age. Over the years since then, while living and working in many foreign lands, I have become increasingly aware of how blessed is the United States of America, and I have developed a deep appreciation for the marvelous freedoms our nation affords us.

During our nation's relatively brief history, we have been continually engaged in a battle to determine, as Abraham Lincoln put it, "whether any nation so conceived . . . can long endure." The American flag is a symbol not just of freedom, but of that ongoing struggle.

Since September 11, 2001, Americans have become aware of new threats to that freedom. The essence of the terrorist attacks on America is an attempt to deny us our freedoms and ultimately to destroy our entire way of life. The security that we have always taken for granted within our borders has been challenged and we are involved in an internal struggle to ascertain how many of our individual freedoms we must curtail to assure our security. It is not an easy choice in a land founded upon the basic principle that a free people can come and go as they choose.

As many of our patriots have warned us, freedom isn't free! An old adage? Perhaps. But it seems that each succeeding generation needs to relearn the concept. Fortunately, Americans' commitment to the ideal of freedom appears to still be burning bright. We still have heroes who will put their lives on the line to safeguard this treasure for us and our posterity. We still have men and women who will 'stand on the wall' and shout to the invaders, *"Not on MY watch will you harm this people."*

If I have learned anything from the telling and retelling of this story, it is that our need to be free, our national will to survive, indeed our strength to endure can flourish only under a system of free choice, such as granted by our gracious God. It is by the principles He has taught, and in the light that He brings, that we find true peace . . . even in time of turmoil.

I am reminded of one of the essential principles that should guide us as a nation. It is reputed to have been voiced by President Abraham Lincoln, who, during the Civil War was asked, "Mr. President, do you think God is on our side in this conflict?"

Lincoln is reported to have replied, "My concern is not whether God is on our side, but whether or not we are on *His* side."

Threads of Honor is my expression of gratitude to those who have sacrificed to perpetuate the American dream. We owe a lot to such people. And if I might take a moment to offer a personal tribute, I would express my appreciation, indeed my admiration for the primary character of this story, Major William Tolbert. Many have been the professional and spiritual successes of this remarkable man whom I call friend. And it is to his credit that among his greatest memories remains the time he spent in formative development of these young Boy Scouts. With such men to lead our youth in paths of righteousness, to raise the "Title of Liberty" upon its standard and wave it for all the world to see, it is no wonder the future looks bright.

It is my hope that this little book will enhance our reverence for our flag, remind us of our heritage, and help ensure in some small way the preservation of our way of life, so that we may always have the right to "Let freedom ring."

Gordon W. Ryan
Christchurch, New Zealand
April 2003

PROLOGUE

While waiting to give his speech, Major Bill Tolbert sat on the dais and gazed out over the large audience. It was April 6, 1991, and he had been invited to address those in attendance at the western universities' award banquet held at the U.S. Air Force Academy in Colorado Springs. This patriotic speech would later win national honors from the Freedoms Foundation at Valley Forge. As the ceremonies began, Major Tolbert reflected on the events that had brought him to this point. Even now, what had transpired seemed incredible to him. And he hoped he could somehow convey the story to those who were waiting to hear him. He wondered, as he had a thousand times, how he had been so fortunate as to be involved. And he marveled at the way the story had ended.

But was it the end? Several times he had felt that the story had played itself out, only to see a new chapter unfold. Perhaps, his instincts told him, the earlier struggle was only the preparation, the crucible through which all of them had to go to appreciate the meaning behind the flag—indeed, to recognize the threads of honor that they now treasured in their hearts.

Standing now at the podium, Bill exhaled slowly and began his address:

"Tonight, I want to share an amazing story with you. It's a story about the adventure and drama of the American space program. And it's a story about a group of Boy Scouts and the ways they came to understand courage, sacrifice, and faith. But most of all, it's the story of an ordinary American flag — a flag that because of unusual circumstances became very special to those whose lives it touched.

"I was an Air Force officer, assigned to the new Air Force Space Command…"

THREADS OF
HONOR

TENDERFOOT

I was crafted in Spring City, Pennsylvania at the Valley Forge Flag Company. I can't really pinpoint my first conscious thought, but I believe it came as my fiftieth star was being stitched. Shortly thereafter, I clearly remember someone hemming my edges and installing two brass grommets— one up top near the blue field and one toward the corner of my bottom stripe.

That first night, after my fabrication was complete and the building fell silent, I listened with interest to the chatter of my older brothers and sisters as they speculated about their forthcoming assignments. Then the conversations suddenly ceased.

An enormous American flag unfurled himself from the ceiling and hung majestically before us. Then he began to speak in a deep, sonorous voice.

"Who's that?" I whispered to my older sibling, who lay folded neatly on the shelf next to me.

"Shush," he whispered back. "That's the Flag Master— the Keeper of the Sacred Thread."

"Oh," I replied and listened.

I was astonished at the Flag Master's enormity and impressed by the authority with which he addressed us. He spoke with great feeling about the history of our nation and explained that each of us would go from that place to an assignment that would be uniquely ours. He emphasized the responsibility that was ours—to fly with dignity and a sense of honor.

Then he said that some of us would journey to Washington, D.C. There, we would begin our service in a brief but glorious moment. It would be our privilege to be hoisted on a staff mounted on the roof of the Capitol Building. After flying briefly there, we would be reassigned. Each of us could look forward to a lifetime of service, with the added prestige of having been a "United States Capitol flag."

My last night at the Valley Forge Flag Company I gathered the courage to ask the Flag Master if he knew my destiny. With a slight ruffle of his edges, he looked down at my small, four-by-six-foot stature and, speaking with a voice that seemed to reverberate through eternity, answered in a way that inspired me, but also puzzled me a little.

"I know your history young man, but your destiny is in your threads. See that you honor them."

Bill Tolbert steered into his driveway, activated the remote-control garage-door opener and inched forward until the tennis ball dangling from the ceiling of the garage just touched his windshield. Grabbing his briefcase, he took the stairs two at a time and entered the bedroom. He was hanging his uniform jacket when his wife, Chris, came into the room. She smiled as she handed him a glass of orange juice.

"Tough night?" she asked.

"Not bad," he replied, "But guess what they asked me to do?"

"Be the new scoutmaster," Chris said, matter-of-factly.

"How did you know?"

"Jackie told me."

Bill grinned. "The wives always know first, don't they?" Chris just smiled.

"I'm worried about it, Chris," Bill went on. "It'll take a lot of time and with my new assignment at work, I'm not sure I can do it."

"I know you can do it, Bill. It'll be good for you, I know it will," she said. "Besides, you'll be great with the boys."

"How is it that a wife always knows what's good for her husband and it's always something other than golf?"

"That's why God made us," she smiled. "So our husbands would always do what's good for them."

Bill pulled off his tie, half hearing Chris's remarks, and sat on the edge of the bed to remove his shoes. "I'll give it a night's sleep," he mumbled, mostly to himself.

Ten minutes later as Bill was drifting off to sleep, Chris turned to him, draping her arm over his shoulder and snuggling up to his back. "Bill?" she whispered.

"Ummm?"

"Bill, I know you're the one for the job."

Bill rolled over on his back, Chris laying her head on his chest as he laced his fingers through her hair. "Chris, I've got seventeen men and women in my division waiting for me to give them directions each day and a colonel who thinks I'm too young and inexperienced, waiting to evaluate how I do it. According to the general, I'm also the one for *that* job."

"Maybe these six young men need you too," she replied.

Bill considered her comments for a moment. "You know, I never got past Second Class when I was a scout."

They lay quietly in the dark for a few moments.

"Bill Tolbert, Scoutmaster," he pronounced, in an official tone.

"Sounds good to me, Major Tolbert," she chided.

"Maybe," he said, rolling back over to go to sleep. "We'll see what the colonel says in the morning. He may not think it's such a hot idea."

"You're the man for the job, Bill," Chris said again, turning toward the window and watching through the drapes as the moon rose over the trees in the Black Forest Estates near Colorado Springs. "*And the boys may teach you more than you teach them,*" she thought as she closed her eyes.

"Morning, Major," Lieutenant Jack Henry called out across the parking lot. "My son tells me you're gonna be his new Scoutmaster. Boy, that's a relief. I thought they'd hook me into it."

Sliding out from behind the wheel, Bill locked his car and began to walk toward his office, the young lieutenant saluting and falling in alongside. "Bad news travels fast—is that it?" Bill asked.

"Something like that, I suppose," his friend laughed.

"Well, if, and I said *if*, I accept the job, the first thing I'll need is a willing 'gofer' as my assistant scoutmaster. Know anyone qualified, Lieutenant?" Bill grinned at him.

"Not a one, Sir. Not a one," he dodged. "Better run, Major. I've got to get that flight estimate for your morning staff meeting with the colonel."

As they entered the building, Lieutenant Henry turned down the hall and hurried toward his office. "You do that Jack," Bill called after him.

Turning into his office, Bill checked the fax and passed his secretary's desk. "Morning, Mary. Have a good weekend?"

"I did, Major. Oh, and Major, the general's secretary telephoned earlier. Colonel Addison's been called away. General Kitchner will chair the staff meeting this morning."

"Thanks, Mary. Call Lieutenant Henry if you would and let him know. Also remind him to have his presentation slides up and ready to go before nine."

Following staff meeting, Bill lingered as other division chiefs departed. Then he made his way toward General Kitchner who noticed him coming and smiled. "Good briefing, Major."

"Thank you, Sir. General, with Colonel Addison gone for a couple of weeks, I need to obtain permission for an outside assignment. I don't believe it will interfere with my duties here, Sir, but thought the colonel should concur."

Kitchner's eyebrows raised slightly as he waited for Bill to continue.

"Sir, I've been asked to lead a small Boy Scout troop — a new troop actually. Just six boys.

"Major," Kitchner continued to smile, "ever had the pleasure before?"

"No, Sir."

"I think it will be compatible. Leave a short memo for Colonel Addison about our discussion."

Bill hesitated briefly. "Sir, the colonel has, uh, expressed some concern about the division's workload, my being so new and all."

"Leave the colonel to me, Major. I know he thinks you're young, but Addison's a good man and when he comes to know you, you'll do fine."

"Thank you, General," Bill replied. Retrieving his briefing papers, he departed.

As General Kitchner was gathering up his notes, Lieutenant Henry, who was closing the slide projector and clearing away the equipment, spoke up. "Boy, I was afraid they'd grab me for that one, General."

"Excuse me, Lieutenant?"

"The Scout troop, Sir. I thought they might ask *me* since my son's in the troop. I hope the Major can juggle it."

"You're right out of the academy, aren't you, Lieutenant? How long have you been with us now?"

"About three weeks, Sir."

"And working for Major Tolbert?"

"Just two weeks, Sir."

"Lieutenant, have you ever wondered why I appointed a new major as division chief in what normally is a senior colonel's slot?"

Henry hesitated, not certain how to answer. "No, Sir. I hadn't given it much thought."

"Well, when you can figure that out, son, then you'll know why someone also asked him to lead the scout troop. Carry on, Lieutenant."

"Yes, Sir."

SECOND CLASS

After arriving at the Capitol Building, I sat on the shelf for more than two months while those around me were being chosen to proudly fly and then were sent off for their assignments to the organizations that had requested them. The Flag Master hadn't told us we'd just sit and feel useless. I became impatient. Would I ever get the chance to take the breeze?

The first meeting of Troop 514, Monument, Colorado was held on a warm July evening in the multi-purpose room of the L.D.S. Church. Major Tolbert, anxious to set the example for his fledgling Scouts, greeted the boys completely outfitted in a scoutmaster's uniform. The boys showed up in their school clothes, except for one boy who was wearing a too-small Scout shirt.

As the boys filtered in, Bill greeted them and tried to make them feel comfortable. Several boys knew each other from school or church and they instantly gathered together while the new boys sat apart. In total, Troop 514 consisted of six young men, ranging in age from twelve to fifteen. Only one of the boys, fifteen-year-old Trent Jefferies, had been a Scout before. Trent had reached Star rank. The other boys would all be starting at the bottom of the ladder.

A couple of dads had come along to see what the new scoutmaster was like. Fearing recruitment, the other fathers stayed away.

Bill stood quietly before the boys and surveyed the group, smiling at each young man before he spoke. "Welcome to Troop 514, Scouts." A few nodded acknowledgment of his welcome, but most of the boys remained quiet, unsure of themselves in their new role. Bill moved to the front of the gathering. He paused until they all looked at him, at which point he came to attention, rendered a snappy Scout salute, and began:

"On my honor, I will do my best to do my duty to God and my country . . . "

For the next six months, with Trent assisting as patrol leader, Bill Tolbert worked to unite his diverse group of boys and to identify some common goals and interests. He quickly earned their admiration and friendship, and his recruitment efforts paid off as the troop grew. By the beginning of the following year, four more boys had joined the troop.

Bill had committed to personally pick up four of the boys who didn't have reliable transportation, and each week the Tolbert shuttle made the rounds to their homes before and after troop meetings. Weekends often brought campouts. Twice he took the boys camping in the snow. Bill began to get a sense of satisfaction as he watched the boys come together as friends while they developed an interest in earning merit badges and achieving rank advancements.

In an attempt to identify something that would further unify the Scouts, Bill asked Colorado Congressman Ken Kramer to obtain for the troop a flag that had flown over the United States Capitol. And on a brisk day in February, the package arrived at Bill's home to await the next troop meeting.

As the meeting commenced, the boys quickly sensed that something special was in the air. Departing from their usual ritual, Bill had arranged the scout room in presentation format and had a slide projector set up, with a screen at the front of the room. One by one, without direction from Bill, the boys took their seats.

When the back door opened and Mrs. Tolbert came in with her arms full of small bags of popcorn, the boys let out a cheer and began clapping. Standing at the front of the group, Bill just smiled as Chris passed out the popcorn. Remaining quiet, Bill waited for the boys to settle down.

"What is a symbol?" Bill asked the boys.

"A musical instrument you bang together?" one of the boys asked.

"No," Bill said, "I mean S-Y-M-B-O-L." He wrote the letters on a small chalkboard mounted to the wall.

"You mean like a math symbol?" one asked.

"Well, kind of like that. But I'm asking who knows how symbols are used and why they are important. What does a symbol mean?"

The same youth responded, "Math symbols stand for something. Like 'pi' and we know what it means, uh, so we can, well, you know, uh, we just know it."

The boys laughed at his inability to verbalize his explanation. One of the rowdier boys said sarcastically, "Nice try, Anderson!"

"Don't laugh too quickly," Bill chided. "Dick's right. 'Pi' stands for a long number which all mathematicians know. Rather than spelling out the entire number each time they wish to insert it into an equation, they can save considerable time and writing space by just using the symbol. But beyond math symbols, what else can we think of that symbolizes something?"

"The Golden Arches," Hank yelled out, to the chorus

of teenage laughter. Even Bill couldn't help chuckling.

"Yeah, the 'Big Mac' symbol," Hank added.

"That's true too," Bill said. "The Golden Arches is a symbol of McDonald's Restaurant. When we see that symbol, we know what it represents. That symbol translates into standards you can expect to find."

"And eat," added Jimmy, the troop chow hound.

"And you can sure do that well," Tim retorted amid growing laughter.

Bill waited for the laughter to die down, and then he continued.

"Each of those are good examples of what I'm talking about. Tonight I want to show you another symbol—a symbol that, as Scouts, you've come to respect and one which, by its service to our nation deserves a place of honor."

Bill stopped for a moment and retrieved a brown package from his briefcase, and unwrapped it while the boys watched. The red, white and blue colors appeared quickly and the boys recognized the tri-cornered fold of the American flag.

"Hey, we got our flag! Major Tolbert, that's our troop flag, right?"

"That's right Jeremy. This is the flag we requested from the Capitol. But before we accept it into the troop and present the colors, I want you to watch a brief slide show. We can talk about the symbols in the show, and perhaps gain an understanding of why so many men and women have sacrificed for this flag."

Bill asked one of the boys to flip off the lights, then he turned on the slide projector.

The first slide showed a flag flying over the Capitol Building in Washington, D.C. "This is the history of our personal flag. It has actually flown over the United States

Capitol, and for that brief moment, it represented the United States of America.

"This flag," Bill said, holding up the folded flag in the beam of light from the projector, "once represented America. It will forever carry that honor.

"These other flags," he said, continuing the slide show, "also represented America but they have the added honor of having been present at important moments in American history. Each occupied a unique place during one of those critical moments, and though most of these events took place before any of you were born, they are all part of our nation's heritage, and you need to know about them."

As the images flashed onto the screen, the boys began to shout their knowledge of particular flags. Bill narrated the show.

There was an artist's rendition of the flag flying over Fort McHenry during the War of 1812. Bill reminded the Scouts that it was there, on the deck of a British warship, that Francis Scott Key wrote the poem that later became the words to our national anthem.

There was a slide of the famous photograph of war-weary American marines raising the flag on Mount Suribachi during the battle of Iwo Jima in the Second World War.

In another slide, a tattered American flag flew over the White House on August 14, 1945, the day the Japanese accepted unconditional surrender at the end of World War II. Bill explained to the troop that this particular flag had also flown over Pearl Harbor the morning our military installations were attacked and so many Americans had lost their lives.

Another slide showed Mike Eruzione, a member of the U.S. Olympic ice hockey team, wrapped in an American flag, skating jubilantly around the rink with his teammates after the underdog U.S. team defeated the highly favored Soviet team and took the Gold Medal in the 1980 Winter Olympics at Lake Placid, New York.

There was also a slide showing an elementary class pledging allegiance to the flag at the beginning of their school day.

For twenty minutes, Bill conducted a simple but moving review of American history, showing where, on so many occasions, the stars and stripes had been present to lend dignity or meaning to the occasion.

Bill allowed the final picture to remain for a moment on the screen for a few moments without comment. Finally, one of the boys at the rear of the room asked, "That's you, isn't it Brother Tolbert? Over in the rear?"

"Yes it is, Jeremy. This is a picture of my father's funeral and the flag draped over his coffin in recognition of his service to America during World War II. Many of his friends died during that war, and their coffins were also draped with flags. My mother was presented with my father's flag after his funeral, and she keeps it as a treasured memento. What I want you to remember is that hundreds of thousands of these folded flags rest in as many homes across our nation—reminders to those remaining in those households that someone in that family has served their nation."

"Will you have a flag on your coffin?" Alex asked, again to the laughter of the class.

"Not too soon I hope, Alex," Bill smiled. "But one day, yes, I'm sure I will. Okay, Trent, will you lead us in welcoming our flag to Troop 514 with all due respect and honor."

The boys had learned the ceremony of presenting the colors and once the room had been cleared of screen, projector and popcorn remains, Troop 514, most of them now in full uniform, came to attention. They retired the American flag they had been using. Then, honoring their new flag with appropriate ceremony, they placed it into service, mounted on a stand at the front of the room, to the right of the Colorado State flag which had graced their meetings since the troop was organized.

"Troop, atten-hut. Hand salute," Trent called out and the boys, now well disciplined in the custom of the troop, came to their feet. Rendering a proper salute, Troop 514 remained at attention and concluded the brief ceremony:

"I pledge allegiance to the flag of the United States of America and to the republic for which it stands, one nation, under God, indivisible, with liberty and justice for all."

Given their scoutmaster's connection to the American space program, it was only natural that the members of Troop 514 would develop a focus on aviation. Over the months, Major Tolbert managed to arrange several trips for the young men to a variety of Air Force facilities, including a couple of space laboratories and a flight simulator. Two of the boys even took up astronomy as a personal interest.

Their experience in the flight simulator was particularly fascinating for the young Scouts. They were all intrigued by high-speed flight. In particular, they learned how easy it was for a careless pilot to "crash and burn." Drawing on this lesson, Bill was able to emphasize the importance of paying attention to the details of a job, especially when your own and others' lives hang in the balance.

Major Tolbert's duties at the Space Command kept him in frequent contact with NASA officials and with various astronauts who often came to Colorado on training missions. Some of these visiting astronauts agreed to talk to his young charges, providing the boys with an up-close look at men and women they viewed as authentic American heroes.

While Bill felt the troop was coalescing and beginning to work as a team, he felt the boys still needed something to instill a greater feeling of pride in their unit. He began to wonder if he could arrange to have their troop flag flown on a space shuttle mission. When he brought up the possibility at a troop meeting, the boys were wildly enthusiastic.

The quest had begun.

FIRST CLASS

For more than two months I had been languishing on the shelf in the basement of the Capitol Building. Had I been forgotten? Would I ever be put into service? Then, my day finally came. I was taken out of storage and carried with several of my peers up to the roof of the Capitol. My journey was about to begin!

I knew I'd have only a few precious moments to fly above the Capitol, and I wanted to savor every detail. The winter day was cold but sunny. I was third in line. Suddenly, the hooks were linked to my grommets, and I was hauled swiftly upward on the halyard. Reaching the top of the staff, I hung helplessly, straining to unfurl myself but unable to do so. I longed to see the streets and monuments that lay below me, stretching away into the distance, but I lacked the power to move.

Then I felt the stirring of the wind. My courage growing, I gathered my colors in anticipation, and suddenly my whorls were filled and I took flight! My red and white stripes and my blue field of white stars made their first appearance. I tugged against the halyard and was thrilled to hear my crisp new edges snap in the brisk wind. Far below and halfway down the National Mall, I could see the tall, white Washington Monument. In the distance, the Lincoln Memorial was clearly visible. Flying smartly in the breeze, high above Washington, D.C., I was filled with a sense of joy and pride, and I recalled the Flag Master's challenge to "fly with dignity and a sense of honor." I was exhilarated and felt I had finally begun to fill my destiny.

But then, too soon, it was ended. I was hauled back down the staff, unhooked, and folded neatly. Though I had flown only briefly above the Capitol, I would forever keep the memory of having first taken the breeze in such a place—high above the seat of government of the nation that had been founded on the principles of liberty and justice for all, and looking over the monuments that had been erected to the founders and heroes of that nation.

The Flag Master had told us that if we were fortunate enough to be assigned to a military unit or Scout troop, we would always be treated with the respect he felt we deserved. I was grateful for such an assignment, for it wasn't many days until I was delivered to a Scout troop in Colorado. Before I was put into service, the scoutmaster explained to the young men what I symbolized and reviewed the many places where my forebears, other American flags, had been a part of our history. Lying on the table in that meeting, I swelled with pride. I was grateful to have found such an honorable home and wondered if the others in my Valley Forge class had been so fortunate.

The process that Bill Tolbert was required to go through in his attempt to obtain flight clearance for Troop 514's flag would have deterred a lesser man. But the responsibility he felt for those young men, now numbering fourteen scouts, and the image of their eager faces at each meeting, kept him going. Their excitement over the possibility that *their* flag might actually go into space and return inspired him to persist. He enlisted the help of all his resources to get the flag included in the official flight kit. Finally, beaming with satisfaction, he stood one night before the troop and announced that their request had been approved. Troop 514's flag would be on the next shuttle mission, due to launch in eight weeks.

The next few weeks saw a burst of energy in the troop. There was a renewed interest in the American space program. The boys pored over NASA materials. They learned the names of the astronauts and their career histories. Their familiarity with space jargon grew to rival that of Bill's staff members at the fledgling Space Command at Falcon Air Force Station.

With less than two weeks to go until liftoff, the boys' excitement was palpable. They held their regular troop meeting on Tuesday. However, Tim, Bill's son, kept to himself. He knew what his dad was about to announce.

As the meeting came to order, Bill told the boys he had an announcement to make.

"I'm afraid I have some bad news, Scouts," he began. Immediately a hush fell over the group and all eyes were on Bill. "I received a call from NASA this week." The room was totally quiet. Bill paused again. He had some difficulty saying what he knew he needed to say, because he knew what it would do to the spirits of his troop. "They told me that because of space and weight considerations, our flag will not be able to be carried on this space shuttle mission."

Senior Patrol Leader Trent Jeffries was the first to speak up. "Well, we'll just have them put it on the next mission. That'll be okay. We can just wait a couple of months."

"It's not that simple," replied Bill. "I asked NASA if they could just put the flag on the next shuttle, and they told me that we'd have to start the application process from the beginning."

"That took *months!*" said one of the boys in the back.

"Yes, it did," said Bill, "but we can do it."

His determination didn't appear to be felt by the boys.

The pall cast over the gathering was obvious. His happy group of Scouts was quickly transformed into a glum-looking group. Bill had expected to see dejection, and had planned ahead to try to lift their spirits.

"I've ordered some Domino's pizzas," he announced. The pizzas were delivered, and for a few moments, as they downed them, the Scouts seemed to forget their discouragement. The somber atmosphere, however, quickly returned.

The following meeting found Bill enthusiastic and ready with his plan for another application to NASA. The Scouts didn't share his enthusiasm, and only seven showed up for the meeting. Bill consoled himself by recalling that he had started out a year earlier with only six Scouts. So he set to work enlisting the help of those who came in preparing the application.

For nearly five months the troop plowed through seemingly endless paperwork. Bill saw it as an opportunity to teach the art of persistence to his not always enthusiastic Scouts. But persistence was something Major Tolbert understood. It was an attribute he had acquired in his own quest for achievement.

William Austin Tolbert, from Daly City, California, married his high school sweetheart while they were both still in their teens. Recognizing the educational opportunities afforded by the military, he had enlisted in the Air Force shortly after graduation from high school, and he and his bride had set out to conquer the world. With the financial support of the Air Force, Bill enrolled in college courses. Excelling there, he was ultimately accepted into the Airman Education and Commissioning Program.

With a bachelor's degree in engineering under his arm, academic honors on his record, and gold second lieutenant's bars on his shoulders, Bill quickly accepted an offer from the Air Force to pursue a master's degree in aeronautical engineering. His rise through the ranks was rapid, hindered only by the fact that he had spent nearly ten years as an enlisted man, a circumstance that had robbed him of many opportunities afforded younger officers.

Finally earning his commission in his late twenties, Bill often felt thwarted by his inability to overcome this late start in a system designed to reward seniority more readily than competence. Then, as he approached his twenty-year mark, Bill began to see opportunity in other quarters and considered leaving the Air Force. It was during this unsettled time in his life that the burden of leading a Scout troop was thrust upon him. The demands on his time—the camping trips, meetings, and administrative responsibilities—added to his frustration and diminished his ability to focus on his career and family.

In the midst of this midlife career crisis came the news that Boy Scout Troop 514's flag had been accepted a second time for flight on a space shuttle.

Bill went to the troop meeting, excited to deliver this news. "Well, boys," he told them proudly, "it's taken months to get through this application red tape, but our efforts have been rewarded. If there's one thing I'd like you to learn from this process, it's that persistence does indeed pay off."

"Can we have a party to celebrate?" asked one of the boys.

"We'll have a big party on the day of the liftoff. How's that?" announced Bill.

The Scouts accepted that plan and began discussing the menu. Bill felt happy over the way things had turned out. The flag would see a shuttle mission, and the Scouts had learned a valuable lesson in persistence.

Their jubilation was short-lived. Once again, a couple of weeks before the scheduled liftoff date, the flag was bounced from the flight. Handling the disappointment of his young Scouts was just one more thing to deal with, at a time when Bill felt he didn't need any more problems.

STAR

My brief but thrilling experience flying over the United States Capitol had inspired me. And my arrival in Colorado to begin service to Troop 514 of the Boy Scouts of America had imbued me with a sense of purpose. I hoped I was sufficiently prepared to serve with honor in the gatherings of these young men and their leaders.

I was pleased to think that I could be of service to these scouts and live out my life in their company. I compared myself to many of my peers who had become victims of those who seemed to take pleasure in burning them and belittling the things for which we all stood. There was maybe some peculiar honor to dying the death of a martyr, as these, my fellow flags, had done. But I had visualized for myself a much more noble ending to my life.

My two trips to the Kennedy Space Center had served to heighten my feelings of self-worth. But being twice rejected for flight aboard the spacecraft created in me a sense of shame. I felt diminished, and I returned each time to the troop feeling I had somehow failed in my determination to serve with honor.

That shame, for I saw rejection from the official flight kit as such, became also a source of embarrassment as I crossed paths with my cousins at various Scout and civic activities. Those flags, some born elsewhere from my origins, had neither the prestige of having flown over the United States Capitol, nor the hoped-for promise of space flight, yet neither had they been rejected at the threshold of success.

I wondered again about my destiny and the words of the Flag Master. What did he mean by saying that my destiny was in my threads? And how would I be able to honor them?

"Major Tolbert, General Kitchner's secretary called to inform you of an appointment with the general at three this afternoon."

Bill immediately stood and walked from behind his desk to the doorway between his office and Mary's cubicle. "Did she say what it is about?"

"No, Sir. Just the time for the appointment."

Reaching behind the door for his hat, Bill left for lunch, deciding to run home quickly and pick up some celestial navigation charts for the scout meeting later that evening.

"This is a nice surprise, Bill," Chris said, as he arrived home. "Care for a sandwich?"

"Yeah, thanks. I'll just run upstairs and get some charts I need for tonight."

"Soup too?" she asked.

"No, thanks. Just a sandwich and a glass of milk will be fine."

Chris quickly made Bill a sandwich and set another place at the table in the breakfast nook, next to a window that looked out into a forested area behind the house. She was seated, nibbling on her own half–eaten sandwich when Bill came back downstairs and sat down at the table. "How's your day going?" she asked.

"Ummm," Bill mumbled, taking a bite of sandwich. "Not sure yet. I've got to see General Kitchner this afternoon."

"What for?" Chris asked, her interest rising.

"Don't know that, either."

Aware that generals seldom called majors in for a friendly chat, Chris sat quietly as Bill finished his lunch and then picked up his charts to leave.

"Bill," she said, reaching up to kiss his cheek. "Do you know that I love you? And your children love you. And your scouts love you."

Bill began to smile. He knew Chris' methods. "And I'm sure General Kitchner loves you too," she added, giving him a big hug and a pat on the rump as he went out the door.

"The general may love me, Chris . . ." Bill said as he slid into his car. Then, driving around the circular driveway and stopping momentarily in front of Chris, who stood smiling at him from the porch, he added, ". . . but I doubt he's called me in to pass him off on his merit badges."

"Major, the general will see you now."

Bill rose from his upholstered chair in the general's foyer and walked briskly into his office. Approaching and coming to attention eighteen inches from the desk, he focused his eyes straight ahead, at a spot directly over General Kitchner's head. "Sir, Major Tolbert reporting as ordered."

General Kitchner looked up from his papers, and permitted a hint of a smile to cross his face. "Sit down, Major. What's the good word from your division?"

"Wheel's up, Sir, and gaining airspeed and altitude all the time."

Kitchner laughed and leaned forward on his desk. "About what I'd expect. Tell me, Major, why do you think I appointed you to that slot—what is it now, about a year ago?"

Bill was surprised by Kitchner's question, and wasn't quite certain how to respond. "Sir, I assumed the general used the resources at his command until someone more qualified was transferred in."

"Well, it's been over a year, hasn't it, Major? If that's the case, why haven't I put this 'more qualified' person in your place?" he pressed.

"Sir, I'm not certain of the general's motives. A training program perhaps, or maybe . . ."

"Listen, Bill," Kitchner said, offering informality which Bill knew was not meant to be reciprocated, but which signaled that Bill was not in trouble, "I could have put a qualified colonel in that slot at any time this past year, and left you in as his deputy. But what would that gain me? It's a new division—in fact a whole new command here at Falcon. Unless I was really lucky, I'd have gotten a nineteen year's service colonel looking for a place to R.I.P. until his time to punch out."

Bill smiled at the generals use of "retire in place"—the military's tongue-in-cheek term for those who merely sit around, waiting for their twenty years to expire.

"I put you there, Bill, because I've seen your work and because I called your last boss. You don't quit and you get the best out of your troops because you care about them, just the way you do about those young Boy Scouts of yours."

Kitchner watched as Bill's surprise showed on his face. "That's right, Major. I get reports on all activities on or near this base. That's my job. But, what I'm saying is, you're in that slot because I wanted the division to get up and running fast, and I wanted you to run it because, well, because in spite of the offense it paid to more senior officers, it's kept them on their toes, hasn't it?"

"Well, sir, I'm not sure I can judge that . . ."

"Of course you can't, Major. It was a rhetorical question. Just believe me. It has."

General Kitchner had been seated somewhat informally in his large swivel chair, facing sideways. Now he turned and leaned forward to look intently at Major Tolbert.

"But I've been hearing rumors that you might be looking over the fence at what may appear to be greener grass on the other side. You've got a promising career ahead of you in the Air Force, son, and I'd hate to see you throw it away."

"Sir, may I speak candidly?"

"Absolutely, Major. Speak your mind."

"I feel like I'm behind the eight ball, General. I got a late start, considering my enlisted time and all. To use an old cliché, 'I don't think I can get there from here.'"

"Where is it you want to get, Major?"

Bill was silent for a moment, a slight smile playing at the corners of his mouth.

"Stars on your collar, eh?" Kitchner grinned. "Can't blame you son. They're the only thing worth seeking in this man's air force. I'll tell it to you straight, Major. I can't promise you that you'll get a star on your shoulder if you stay. A lot of factors play into that, and much of it is beyond our control. Some fine officers have never made it, and some . . . well, you know that part, I guess.

"I can tell you one thing, though. You're general officer material and given the right place, at the right time, with the right support, it *will* happen. I could see that potential, and that's why I put you in that division—in spite of whatever resentment it might create."

As General Kitchner rose and came around his desk, Bill also stood. "Give it some thought son, and don't be hasty with your decision. Understood?"

"Understood, General. And thank you, Sir."

"Glad to be of help, son. We need young tigers in the Air Force as much as any civilian corporation, and getting them over the hurdle of more senior officers who are content to R.I.P. is a problem, but one we can deal with—sometimes."

As Bill turned to leave, General Kitchner stopped him. "One more thing, Major. I've heard about your disappointments over your Scout troop's flag being bumped from two shuttle missions now. I've got a few favors hanging out there—down at NASA, I mean. Let's see if we can't call in a few chips and give your Scout flag a ride."

"I don't know if the boys are up for another disappointment, General."

Kitchner reached to shake Bill's hand, smiling as he walked him to the door. "Well, then, let's not give them one."

"Okay, whose turn is it to lead us in the Pledge of Allegiance tonight," Bill asked.

The opening services over, Bill asked the boys to take seats so they could begin their monthly business meeting. A fund-raising project and an upcoming camping trip took up the first twenty minutes. Several of the Scouts were commended for work they had done on merit badges, and then Bill jumped into the main item on his agenda.

"Who's up for resubmitting our flag application to NASA?"

Groans and catcalls rose from the majority of the boys in the room. "What for?" one of the boys shouted. "It's never gonna happen," said another. "Three strikes and you're out," yelled Tim, Bill's son.

"Then we're not out yet, are we?"

"Aw, c'mon, Bill," Jeremy said. "It's a waste. Let's do something else. Plant the flag up on Pike's Peak or something. Something we can do for real."

Bill had known the boys would buck him on resubmitting. They had gotten their hopes up twice, only to be disappointed. Still, he wanted them to see the project through. "What'll happen if we don't send the flag back to NASA?"

"Huh?"

"If we don't resubmit, I mean."

"Well it'll stay grounded," John giggled.

"But if we *do*?" Bill pushed.

"They'll just tell us to get lost, Dad. Who needs that?" Tim said, and most of the boys agreed.

"Well, I say we try again," Bill said flatly.

"*You* can," Jeremy challenged.

"I said *we*," Bill stated.

"Why should we?"

"Because that's what the flag is all about. That's one of the things it stands for—never give up. Look, guys, only *you* can quit. What I mean is, only *you* can tell yourselves no. Other people or circumstances can stand in your way and make you find ways around them, but," he looked directly at each of the boys, "only *you* can quit."

"And if they turn us down again . . . what then, Bill, huh?"

"Then we'll try Plan B."

"We're on Plan C already, Bill," Alex put in.

Bill smiled. "You're right, Alex. So it's Plan C and then Plan D."

"And if *they* don't work?"

"There are twenty-six letters in the alphabet," Bill declared, drawing groans from the boys.

"Look guys," Bill said, adopting a more conciliatory tone, "I know it's been discouraging to get bumped twice from shuttle missions. But the decision we made to try was a good one—that hasn't changed. We want our flag to fly on a space shuttle. Right? And getting that to happen hasn't been easy. But I can guarantee you one thing—if we don't try again, it will never fly. If we do try again, it might. Which course offers the possibility of success?"

Most of the boys shook their heads and complained loudly, but some of them were grinning. If nothing else, they had learned by now that if Major Bill Tolbert was determined to do something, he would persevere until he accomplished what he set out to do.

"What do you think, Trent?" Bill asked his senior patrol leader. Trent, who had by now been accepted by the younger boys as a leader, was leaning forward, looking at the floor as most of the troop complained. He looked up at Bill. "My dad said the same thing, Bill. I say we go for it."

"All right," Jeremy said, "but on *our* conditions."

"And those are?" Bill grinned.

"Pizza's all around if we get bumped again."

"Or two cords of wood cut for me, if we fly," Bill challenged, to another round of groans. "Deal?"

"Deal," several of the boys chorused. "But you might as well order the pizzas now, Bill. We're hungry."

"I think I'll wait awhile," he said.

LIFE

I wasn't sure whether to be thrilled or scared, but once again I found myself being boxed up and shipped to the Kennedy Space Center, Cape Canaveral, Florida. Approval had been granted for me to be included in the official flight kit of NASA Mission 51-L. Once again, the countdown had begun.

Bill tried to keep the boys' enthusiasm in check as they followed the preflight countdown. When they got within two weeks of launch, the point at which they had twice previously been bumped, Bill went to his office each day, dreading the inevitable phone call. To his relief, it never came.

Finally, on the Tuesday night before the scheduled liftoff, the troop was gathered for its weekly meeting.

"The first order of business tonight," Bill began formally, "is to assign woodcutting teams."

The boys stared blankly at Bill until he began to smile.

"Would that be Tolbert's woodpile?" Jeremy asked.

"I thought you guys might like to get a head start," Bill ribbed.

"No way! We've been figuring all along we'd be having pizza."

"I'll tell you what," Bill said, "we'll do both. "Tomorrow

afternoon, after liftoff, we'll chop wood *and* eat pizza. How's that?"

Some of the boys cheered.

"Two cords?" Alex asked. "That's what, two feet by two feet?" he joked.

"Try four feet high, four wide, and eight long—twice," Bill corrected.

"That's bigger than Jimmy," Alex heckled, and set the boys laughing at the reference to the largest member of the troop.

"Yeah, it is," Jimmy retorted, "and I'll eat your share of the pizza before you ever get a hand on it if you keep flappin' your mouth."

"OK, OK, let's get down to business. You're getting out of school early tomorrow, so everyone meet at my house at 1300 hours. Wear your work clothes and bring your appetites. We're about to see history made, guys, and we're part of it. The third time's the charm. It's 'wheels up' and no limits," Bill cried as the scouts whooped it up in anticipation of the big day.

Wednesday morning brought the news that the shuttle liftoff had been postponed. The previous mission, the *Columbia*, which was supposed to have launched on December 18, 1985, had several mechanical delays followed by weather delays, and didn't actually launch until January 12. Then, the return had to be delayed several times due to persistent bad weather. It ended up having to land at Edwards Air Force Base in California on January 18. Shuttle mission 51-L, the mission that was to carry Troop 514's flag, was postponed a day, then another day, and then another. Bill kept in touch with his Scouts with each postponement. Plans now were to meet on Saturday, January 25, which looked like it was a "go" for a launch date. However, bad weather at the transoceanic abort landing site forced two more postponements and switching to a morning launch time. Then Monday morning the ground servicing equipment couldn't be removed from the orbiter hatch. After that was fixed, cross winds had become too severe, and the launch was moved to Tuesday, January 28. The anticipation was becoming agonizing. Hopefully, this was the last postponement.

Tuesday morning, January 28, 1986, seventeen excited Scouts from Troop 514 were gathered in the Tolberts' living room, fighting for space on the easy chairs and couch and settling for the floor when they lost. Chris Tolbert had prepared mounds of snacks, although with seventeen hungry boys, she quickly realized that the field kitchen from the Air Force base would have had trouble satisfying their appetites.

Bill sat quietly in his chair, which Chris had posted with a "reserved" sign before the boys began arriving. He and the boys watched as the astronauts prepared to enter the van that would deliver them to the launchpad, all seven waving and smiling at the television cameras and the assembled dignitaries.

Their anxieties heightened again as mechanical difficulties delayed the launch further. An hour passed, and then another. The boys spent part of the time eating and then began horsing around in the living room. Chris eventually chased them outside onto the snow-covered lawn where they could roughhouse freely. Finally, it was announced that the launch would go forward, and they summoned the boys back to the living room.

Reassembled in front of the television, the perspiring and excited Scouts sat with their eyes glued to the set. The minutes and then the seconds ticked away. At 9:38 A.M., Colorado time, with three seconds to go in the countdown, the huge engines began to fill the television screen with white steam. Then the familiar words emanated from

Mission Control: "Liftoff. We have liftoff." The boys cheered and whistled, driving the Tolberts' Airedale Terrier off the porch and into the woods to escape the noise. Clearing the gantry, Mission 51-L began the slow rotation designed to place the shuttle craft in the proper attitude for the climb to stage-one separation.

Bill sat enthralled, watching both the television and his Scouts. Despite his professional involvement and familiarity with aeronautics, he had never gotten over marveling at the technology that made space flight possible. Added to that was the knowledge that the boys had succeeded in their dream and that their troop flag was somewhere on board the spacecraft.

As he contemplated the rewards of their persistence, the space shuttle *Challenger*, manned by seven of the finest astronauts America had to offer, completed her roll program, commenced first-stage separation . . . and entered history.

For most in the room, understanding came slowly. The separation of the *Challenger* from the rocket that carried it upward and the concussion that accompanied that event looked almost like previous separations. But Bill saw immediately that something had gone horribly wrong. The silence from the television confirmed his fears. Barely a second later, there was an explosion and a huge white cloud where the *Challenger* had been. Dozens of small fragments of the shuttle then shot out in different directions and trailed down to the ocean. The *Challenger* was gone, and, in an instant, seven dedicated Americans died. Commander Francis (Dick) Scobee, Pilot Michael Smith, Mission Specialists Judy Resnick, Ellison Onizuka and Ronald McNair, Payload Specialist Gregory Jarvis and Christa McAuliffe, America's first "teacher in space."

The Scouts were slow to comprehend, but, looking from the television screen to the face of their scoutmaster, they began to realize what had happened. They saw the tears on his face, and, rather than resisting their grief in an awkward teenage effort to be cool, they surrendered to their emotions and joined him in the release of their sorrow — for the crew, for their flag, and for their dream.

For the next hour, the stunned Scouts sat with Bill and Chris Tolbert, contemplating what they had seen and consoling and being consoled by each other. The boys had spent time learning the names of the astronauts assigned to this flight and knew something of their backgrounds. For many of the Scouts, it was their first experience with that kind of agonizing grief, and they struggled to cope with the shock. For them, thinking of their precious flag, it was almost as though eight crew members, rather than seven, had perished on the *Challenger*. For the following hour, as they sat in Bill's living room, these young boy scouts learned first hand the hollow, empty feeling that accompanies deeply felt and uncontrollable grief.

In the hours and days that followed, the American public would learn a great deal about the seven astronauts who had died so suddenly. They were from widely different backgrounds, different cultures, different religions, and different professions. Following a common dream, they had come together as a team to carry the honor, pride, and spirit of their nation into space. In the process, they had been called upon to give what so many of America's heroes have given — their lives in exchange for progress. In that sacrifice, they had achieved a measure of immortality.

The *Challenger* disaster stunned the entire nation. President Reagan addressed the nation later that day. In a brief but eloquent address, he verbalized what all Americans were feeling. Of those who had died, he said,

"We will never forget them, nor the last time we saw them this morning, as they prepared for their journey and waved good-bye, and slipped the surly bonds of Earth to touch the face of God." He ordered that all flags be flown at half-mast, and across the country people struggled to make sense of the tragedy. After so many successful launches, space flight had become routine for most casual observers. The dramatic failure and tragedy reminded everyone of the dangers inherent in attempting to ride powerful rockets into orbit.

General Kitchner held a memorial service in which the military paid fitting and traditional tribute to its fallen heroes. Then the entire command at Falcon Air Force Station and Bill's division responded with renewed determination. Bill returned to work, his Scouts returned to school, and life picked up its routine as duty requires.

Still, no one who watched the launch on television or who saw the replays of the horrifying event would ever forget the shock of seeing the explosion and watching the debris, trailing plumes of smoke, spiraling wildly through the sky.

NASA immediately set about to recover the wreckage from the disaster, hoping to piece together evidence that would show conclusively what had gone wrong. Fragments and huge pieces of the rocket and shuttle were being recovered. With each news report, Bill found himself hoping that the troop flag, or some remnant of it, might somehow be found. He even contacted some of the people he had dealt with in getting the flag placed on board. In the face of the human tragedy that had occurred, he was somewhat embarrassed to inquire about something so worldly as a flag, but he felt compelled.

For weeks and then months, as news of shuttle remnants discovered on the ocean floor made newscasts, Bill sought to contact every person with whom he had dealt in the long, agonizing process to place the flag aboard the *Challenger.* Often, he felt shameless, seeking return of something that was, viewed from the scope of human tragedy, insignificant. Those to whom he spoke all said the same thing: "It probably didn't survive the explosion and fire. If it did, it probably will never be found. If it is found, you probably will never hear about it. If you do, you probably won't ever get it back."

NASA officials were sensitive to the loss felt by Bill and his troop. As a consolation, they offered him a set of small flags that were also supposed to have been included in the official flight kit but were left off. Bill accepted the token gratefully.

It was tough facing it. Everyone who was familiar with NASA told him there was no hope, and eventually, he resigned himself to the loss and began seeking new ways to unify his boys and regenerate their interest in the Scout troop. But it was hard for Bill to try to motivate the Scouts, for he had lost some of his own enthusiasm.

A few weeks after the disaster, Bill organized a memorial service to honor the astronauts who had lost their lives. It was to be part of a troop Court of Honor, and Bill hoped that the event would serve as a sort of closure for his Scouts.

In his remarks to the Scouts, their parents, and others, Bill had a difficult time controlling his emotions. As a gesture of respect for Christa McAuliffe, several of the boys' schoolteachers attended. Bill found it moving that they would come, and remembering Christa's sacrifice and that of the other six astronauts brought back much of the pain everyone had experienced at the time of the disaster.

Most of those attending had some affiliation with either the military or the government, and they felt a party to the loss of the *Challenger* and its crew. Throughout the evening, tears flowed as the Scouts and the others reflected on the sacrifices made by many in service to their country, and on the blessing it is to be an American citizen.

As part of his presentation, Bill presented each boy with one of the small flags he had received earlier from NASA. He challenged each boy to do something special with his individual flag—to take it to Mars with him when it came his turn, to plant it alongside Neil Armstrong's flag on the moon, to stand it beside Sir Edmund Hillary's New Zealand flag on Mount Everest, to take it to the depths of the oceans as he explored new frontiers, or to take it to Congress when he was elected to serve—to make it a symbol of his patriotism and commitment to freedom.

After the meeting, Chris stood at Bill's side as the parents of the boys came forward to thank Bill for the interest he had taken in their sons. Others came to express their appreciation for the memorial service. Though less able to verbalize their feelings, the Scouts also demonstrated their love for their leader by the way they gathered around to have him tousle their hair or trade good-natured punches on the arm.

Observing all this, Chris remembered the night she had discussed with Bill his reluctance to accept the call to become a scoutmaster. The experiences Bill had shared with the members of his troop had enriched the Tolberts' lives, just as Chris had known they would. Bill had grown through the service he had given—and in some ways, the boys had indeed taught Bill more than he had taught them.

Later, Bill lay awake long into the night and by his restless movement, brought Chris to his side.

"Thinking, Bill?"

"I can't shake the feeling, Chris," he replied, continuing the conversation he had shared with her occasionally for the past several weeks.

"You've got to let go, Bill. To believe what you told the boys tonight. Accept the loss of the Challenger as a learning process and move on."

"The flag's still out there, Chris, I know it."

"Maybe, but like they told you, it'll never be found, Bill," she said softly, rising slightly and leaning over to look into his eyes. "Even the families of the astronauts would like to believe, that somewhere, somehow, they could . . ." she faltered, her voice drifting as the thought could not escape her lips.

Bill lay silently for a few moments, content to hold Chris as they understood that they were still united — that each still had the comfort of the other, and seven families across America no longer had that consolation.

"It *is* out there, Chris. I can feel it."

EAGLE

How proud I was as each member of the flight crew took the time to check the Official Flight Kit and touch my stars and stripes. As the countdown continued, and the engines roared to life, I felt the same inadequacy which had nearly overcome me when first I rose the Capitol flagstaff. The noise and vibration were frightening, but my crewmates seemed to take it in stride, so I tried to relax and accept the rough ride.

I never knew what actually happened. There was a tremendous explosion, and it became very hot. The medallions that traveled next to me in a separate container in our locker melted. Once proud symbols themselves, they became only memories and mere lumps of metal. I feared for my own life and wondered if I, too, would become only a memory. Then the vibration ceased, and an eerie silence ensued. For an instant, I saw my crewmates as they were released from earthly bondage, standing together, outlined against the sky, and united in purpose for one last moment. Then, suddenly, they were gone.

I had the sensation that I was falling. My vision dimmed as the waters of the ocean closed over my vacuum-packed, air-tight container, and I drifted gently downward for a long time. Finally, I felt a jolt, and I came to rest.

I was in the dark for a long time. Weeks turned into months. One day, light broke through my plastic wrapping, to find me back in the preflight area at Kennedy Space Center.

When I learned that I was going home again, I thought of
my crewmates . . . and I wept.

As Bill was leaving for work one morning in September
1986, nearly eight months after the *Challenger* disaster, he
leaned over to pick up the morning paper. He glanced at
the headline and felt his heart jump.

"NASA TO RETURN *CHALLENGER* FLAG
TO BOY SCOUT TROOP"

Bill cried out loud in what he later described as an
'uttering of the heart,' and ran back into the house to show
Chris. Placing several calls to his contacts at NASA, he was
able to confirm the report. It was indeed Troop 514's flag.
He had no idea what condition it would be in, but it didn't
matter, it was coming home!

In a ceremony held on December 18, 1986, at Falcon
Air Force Station, Colonel Guy Bluford, an Eagle Scout and
an astronaut in the shuttle program who had flown the
Challenger in its most recent previous mission, stood before
a crowd of well-wishers and presented the recovered flag
to Scoutmaster Bill Tolbert and his beaming boys. From
the Valley Forge Flag Company in Spring City,
Pennsylvania, to the Capitol Building in Washington DC,
to the edge of space in the company of heroes—its red and
white and blue threads somehow unscathed, the official
flag of Boy Scout Troop 514, Monument, Colorado had come
home.

As the flag was reverently unfolded for all to see, it
seemed to Bill a miracle that the flag had survived the fiery
destruction of the *Challenger* and had been recovered from
the ocean floor after all those months, completely intact and

unspoiled. He could almost feel seven pairs of unseen hands assisting in its unfolding and hear the beating of seven invisible hearts as its vivid red, white, and blue colors were presented. Speaking of freedom and the American dream, Major Bill Tolbert responded to the gathering by quoting President Andrew Jackson, "You have the highest of human trusts committed to your care. Providence has showered on this favored land blessings without number, and has chosen you, as the guardians of freedom, to preserve it for the benefit of the human race. May He who holds in His hands the destinies of nations make you worthy of the favors He has bestowed, and enable you, with pure hearts, and pure hands, and sleepless vigilance, to guard and defend to the end of time the great charge He has committed to your keeping."

As they left the auditorium, many, including Bill, felt that the saga was over—that an end to one flag's epic and inspiring journey had been reached.

But the journey was not over, for the story of the flag that wouldn't die had spread.

COURTS OF HONOR

Being back in the hands of my scouts again filled me with love but also with a sense of sorrow. They welcomed me with all their hearts, but yet, I couldn't forget that I alone had survived. As the presentation ceremony began, I felt the presence of my *Challenger* crewmates.

And then I knew why I had been blessed to survive.

I had survived to remind those I met that freedom isn't easily retained—that, like everything of true value in life, it is purchased at a cost. I had survived to serve as a reminder of those who had gone before and who had paid that price. And in my colors was the symbol of what others had given— their loyalty in the blue of my field, their lofty ideals in my fifty white stars, and their courage manifested by their spilt blood in the red of my stripes. I had survived to testify of their sacrifices.

Nineteen-eighty-seven marked the bicentennial of the ratification of the Constitution of the United States. As president of the Constitutional Bicentennial Commission, Chief Justice Warren Burger of the United States Supreme Court designated Troop 514's flag to be the official flag of the Bicentennial celebration. Within days of the flag's story reaching his office, Justice Burger had arranged for an official letter, so designating the flag, to be delivered to Scoutmaster Bill Tolbert.

Shortly thereafter, the members of Troop 514 were selected as Colorado's official delegation to the Bicentennial celebration, and a fund-raising effort was undertaken to help send the troop to Philadelphia.

On 17 September 1987, twenty Scouts and ten leaders from Monument, Colorado, arrived in Philadelphia—as Bill put it, with enough adults to "put a head under each leader's arm to keep the boys' enthusiasm in check." That same day, national news commentator Paul Harvey related the story of the miracle flag on his *Rest of the Story* radio broadcast. He concluded by weeping as he recited the words to "The Star-Spangled Banner," a tribute to another American flag, written in another time. Everywhere Troop 514 went, people wanted to greet the boys and to touch their famous flag.

The members of Boy Scout Troop 514 had the honor of presenting the colors to more than 14,000 Americans who were in attendance at the nationally televised "We the People 200 Constitutional Gala." Standing on the stage of the Civic Center in Philadelphia, Pennsylvania, Bill Tolbert could see Vice President George Bush, the Reverend Jesse Jackson, dozens of senators, members of Congress, and many other government officials in the vast audience. Many celebrities, including actor Jimmy Stewart, were also in attendance—all of them there in recognition of the greatness of the Constitution and in support of America.

Standing there with his boys, it occurred to Bill that Lord Baden-Powell, founder of the Boy Scout movement, would have been pleased with what had transpired and how the ideals he had formulated had affected the young men who were members of Troop 514. Bill later recognized that it was at that moment when he came to truly understand the depth of the Boy Scout oath, "On my honor I will do my duty to God and my country . . ."

Paying homage to the valiant crew of the *Challenger* and describing the events that brought Troop 514's flag to the Constitutional Gala, Bill addressed the audience: "If you were to choose one item to survive the loss of the *Challenger* and its crew, what better than an American flag? And if you were to choose someone to serve as its honor guard, who better than a troop of proud, young Boy Scouts?"

In an effort to capture his feelings, Bill later wrote in his journal:

"Suddenly I found myself standing on a stage with 100 members of the Mormon Tabernacle Choir on either side of me, listening to 100 brass trumpets playing and Sandi Patti singing the most beautiful rendition of "The Star Spangled Banner" that I have ever heard. Looking out at 14,000 people from all walks of American life, all standing with their hands over their hearts and tears in their eyes, filled me with the strangest feeling. I felt the cartilage in my back stretching, and it struck me that I had never stood so tall—that after twenty years in a military uniform, the proudest moment of my life had come while wearing a scoutmaster's uniform, standing beside that flag."

During the next two days, the troop visited the White House and the houses of Congress. Everywhere they went, people expressed admiration for the troop and commended them for their service as guardians of the flag.

Bill took the flag on a personal mission one afternoon. With the assistance of Colorado Congressman Joel Hefley and the cooperation of the Office of the Architect of the Capitol, Bill was able to get the troop flag flown once again above the United States Capitol. He was told by those in charge that, to their knowledge, it was the first time in history that a flag had returned to fly a second time over the Capitol Building.

On the last day of their visit to Washington, D.C., the boys asked Bill if they could go to one more place. They wanted to visit Arlington National Cemetery, where the *Challenger* crew were buried.

It turned out to be an emotionally moving experience for all of them. Bill pointed out the graves of several national heroes but explained that many thousands of other Americans were also buried there—citizens who had simply done their duty as God had given it to them to do.

The Scouts watched from a tree-covered hillside as an impressive ritual unfolded below them. A funeral procession passed by. In the time-honored tradition of military last rites, a horse-drawn caisson bearing a flag-covered casket was followed by a single, riderless horse, with empty boots mounted backward in the stirrups. Behind the horse marched a platoon of young soldiers, moving in measured cadence, the taps on their spit-polished boots clicking smartly on the pavement.

Bill and his young Scouts watched as the procession reached the burial site and came to a halt. After a few moments, the silence was shattered by the reverberation of gunfire from an honor guard of seven riflemen. Each fired three rounds in succession, providing a twenty-one-gun salute for the deceased. Then the boys listened as the solemn strains of "Taps" drifted across the hollow. Two buglers stood a hundred yards apart, on opposing hillsides above the grave site. They played the traditional melody, not quite in unison, creating an echo effect that provided an impressive and stirring conclusion to the service.

Bill noted with satisfaction his Scouts' reverent silence and the serious expressions on their faces. Although these young men were still full of life and energy, they had grown in understanding and had developed the capacity to experience deep feelings and to behave appropriately on solemn occasions.

Walking together under the trees and through the garden of stones, the boys, most of them now Eagle Scouts and all of them wearing their own uniforms, proceeded to the monument that honors the *Challenger* crew. There, the Scouts and their leader unfurled their troop flag and repeated again the Scout Oath:

"On my honor, I will do my duty to God and my country, to obey the Scout Law, to keep myself physically strong, mentally awake, and morally straight."

There were no brass trumpets or choirs—only the silent recognition by a scoutmaster and his scouts of seven brave Americans and an unspoken gratitude for a special flag.

EAGLE PALMS

Memories of the Flag Master ran through my mind as I learned I was to accompany the scouts to Washington DC. Why Providence had granted me the privilege of such an honor I'll never know, but I recalled the words of the Flag Master when I had asked him if he knew my destiny.

"I know your history, young man, but your destiny is in your threads. See that you honor them," he had said.

I felt, once again, inadequate to the task at hand. Circumstances had combined to create my history, and in fact, the *Challenger* herself and my seven crewmates had provided the conditions that had contributed to honors that had been heaped upon me. I thought about my predecessors, whose history the Flag Master had so reverently rehearsed in our lessons. Had they, too, been thrust into the maelstrom that propelled them to honor, and had those with whom they had served been the ones to pay the price?

Then I understood. It was not in my threads that honor resided, but rather in the sacrifices offered by others, whose service has cost them their lives.

Those who had perished on the *Challenger* had contributed. Those young men with whom I had proudly stood on the stage in Philadelphia would yet contribute. It had merely been my privilege to be there at those historic moments, to serve as a symbol of freedom and to focus attention on the greatness of our nation. I had once again flown over the Capitol Building, and with humility in my stars and pride in my stripes, I had paid my respects to my fallen *Challenger* crewmates, waving proudly over their resting place, honoring them, and bidding them a final farewell.

After our return to Colorado, I accompanied Troop 514 to an annual Scout encampment at Camp Alexander, Colorado, under Pike's Peak. There, my history was recounted. I took note of the other troop flags in attendance. They stood tall, listening quietly and reverently to the amazing things I had been privileged to witness. I realized that in the service I had rendered and in those significant moments I had been allowed to serve, I had been the representative of American flags everywhere. Then, by being chosen by our national leaders to be present at the bicentennial celebration of the United States Constitution, my status had changed.

I had become a Flag Master.

The Flag Master at Valley Forge—the Keeper of the Sacred Thread—had been right all along. The honor did indeed reside within my threads, which he knew were a symbol of the diversity of the people, the richness of the culture, the glory of the history, and the beauty of the freedoms that make up the fabric of our nation.

For amber waves of grain made up my threads—and purple mountain majesties made up my threads—and my threads stretched from sea to shining sea. My threads, interwoven with all the other threads, comprised the broad tapestry that is America the Beautiful.

" . . . and that's the story I have to tell you this evening," Bill said, concluding his speech. "Is the journey of the *Challenger* flag complete? Perhaps it is. Perhaps not. All I know is that after these experiences, I perceive the flag differently than I did before. Our flag is much more than a piece of cloth fabricated from red, white, and blue threads.

It is a symbol of the freedoms we enjoy and also a reminder of the sacrifices made by the heroes and patriots who have gone before. We desecrate the flag not only by physically destroying it, but by ignoring the principles upon which this nation was founded or forgetting those who have given their lives in defense of those principles."

Again, as at the beginning of his address, Bill paused and silently looked out at the attentive listeners seated before him, allowing them time to consider the story he had told them.

"Seated among you tonight are Eagle Scouts, future astronauts, future congressmen and congresswomen, and yes," he smiled, "even future scoutmasters. As you look upon this flag tonight and consider its remarkable history, remember that *you* are the threads of red and white and blue that make up the fabric of our country. May you serve with honor."

EPILOGUE

In peace and honor my years passed and I watched as young man after young man from Troop 514 sought for the rank of Eagle Scout. After those heady days at the Nation's Bicentennial Gala, perhaps in some respects I had hoped for tranquility and understanding to gain the upper hand in our world, yet if the lessons were true that the Flag Master, The Keeper of the Sacred Thread, had taught, periods of serenity and harmony were only lulls in the journey of man. Each generation found it necessary to face the turmoil of conflict; some from within themselves, some from those external forces that continue to seek the destruction of our way of life.

After many ceremonies and activities, I have come to a place of peace and harmony in Salt Lake City. I have had a busy life, witnessed memorable events and heroic people, and now I have come to enjoy the opportunity to rest. Lovingly and reverently, I was placed in a glass case where I can look out at many people who come to see me and to learn of those with whom I have served. I have by my side a plaque that was made in honor of my mission. I like to listen to the people, and I hear of many things, many lands, many customs. Sadly, I have learned that seven more of my NASA crewmates entered history as the *Columbia* tragedy once again brought renewed understanding of the price of progress. And I wept!

I have also learned of new threats to the liberty that I symbolize. Great disasters struck our nation in New York City and yes, even in the Nation's Capital where I first took flight. Many innocent people sacrificed their lives and loved ones as evil forces continued their determination to take away our liberty to choose how we live. And again, I wept

Yet how proud I was to hear that in the shattered, twisted metal of those once noble structures, one of my brothers flew proudly above the carnage, hastily raised by courageous rescuers who knew the worth of symbols—and the importance of national dignity. My brother was ripped, his threads torn by those evil forces, but by surviving the explosions and fire, he came also to symbolize what I symbolize—that the love of liberty that exists in the hearts of the people of our nation will endure. Even though America wept, the hearts of the people also leapt within their breasts as their pride was re-kindled in the effort and they became determined to see that the threats to our liberty were defeated, that justice prevailed.

Then, not long after that devastating tragedy, I found further cause for hope, as thousands upon thousands of people, from many nations, many religions, and governments from all over the world, paraded before my display case as the 2002 Winter Olympic Games were hosted in Salt Lake City. I heard the Olympic hosts say they wanted to light the fire within every human being. When they talked about 'lighting the fire within,' I thought about the worth of each individual soul and about the fire of liberty that I symbolize. I felt proud to be a part of that event, and I knew then that through the acts of strong patriots, such as my crewmates, good would eventually triumph over evil. But I also felt certain, shuddering at the thought, that more innocent people would likely succumb to the threat and actions of those who would continue their quest to take away our freedoms.

If some future day we meet, you and I—if I am on display somewhere in Salt Lake City, or Colorado, or our Nation's

Capital, and you find reason to visit me and read my history—please do not think of me as more than merely the symbol for those who have sacrificed to preserve and protect the freedoms which you enjoy. For, as I said some years ago in my youth, in my threads resides their honor.

The *Challenger* Flag
February 2003

THREADS OF RED AND WHITE AND BLUE

Many memories rich and true rest in the heart of a flag, deep within its threads of red and white and blue;

There within its field of stars this humble flag has many memories of tears and cheers, of tragedy and scars;

Memories of its journey from the shining sea to the mountains majesty where it was prepared for a journey into space, and history;

Memories of the day it met the destined crew, seven from different worlds, united in a dream to touch the stars, and the heart of humankind;

Memories of delays and waits until that hour when it began its flight while a country watched;

Memories of the thrill of liftoff and the hope of dreams, the cheers, the rockets red glare, bombs bursting in air, then silence as all fell to earth a different purpose to fulfill;

Memories of storm tossed seas and the quiet of the oceans depths, alone save for seven of the nations best;

Memories of sunlight once again, and cheers, and a journey back to the home of the free and the brave, its destiny again to wave;

Memories of a great parade, where so proudly they hailed in the morning dew, a miracle flag, held tight by the hands of three youth;

Memories of destiny fulfilled at twilight's last gleaming, in a great hall amid the roar of trumpets and the sound of angels voices;

Memories of seven young men, holding it aloft for all to share, giving proof through the night that the flag was still there;

Memories of a journey at last now complete, flying once again over the nation's seat, then onto the vast green fields where generations of freedom's youth rest;

Memories of seeing here, once again, the now resting crew who gave this proud flag its softest memories, and its mission to fulfill for all the world to see;

For eternity there will always be memories rich and true resting in the heart of this great flag, in its field of stars, deep within its threads of red, and white, and blue.

William A. Tolbert, 1987

Note: Bill Tolbert, now retired from the United States Air Force, still lives and works in Colorado. Married for thirty-six years to his high school sweetheart, Chris, and the father of five children, he currently serves as a Senior Vice President of CH2M HILL, an international engineering design and construction firm headquartered in Englewood, Colorado.

Members of Boy Scout Troop 514, who participated in those memorable events in 1986 and 1987, are now in their twenties and thirties, and have gone on to various professions and educational endeavors. They carry in their hearts, as does their Scoutmaster, the memories of a flag that wouldn't die, and the spirit of the nation it represents.

ABOUT THE AUTHOR

Gordon Ryan is a published novelist, a former City Manager, and served in the United States Air Force with Major Tolbert. Ryan is married to Colleen Sterling of Christchurch, New Zealand, where they currently reside. They are the parents of six children and eleven grandchildren.

Threads of Honor was written as a result of Ryan's lifelong friendship with Scoutmaster Bill Tolbert.

If you know of an inspiring flag story, want to comment about this book, or simply want to communicate with the author, he can be reached on the internet. Either visit his web site at www.gordonryan.com or write to him at novelist@xtra.co.nz.

APPENDICES

PHOTO GALLERY

Boy Scout Troop 514 at the National Air and Space Museum in
Washington, D.C.
(Photo courtesy of William Tolbert)

Troop 514 and the *Challenger* flag at the Bicentennial
Celebration, Constitution Hall, Philadelphia, September 17,
1987 (Photo courtesy Don Hoffman)

The *Challenger* flag returned to Troop 514 by
Astronaut Guy Bluford (third from right) at Falcon Air Force Base
(Photo courtesy of U.S. Air Force)

Plaque from NASA in recognition of the *Challenger* flag
(Photo courtesy Bill Tolbert)

January 28, 1986, the crew of the *Challenger* boarding the
shuttle. (Photo courtesy NASA)

The *Challenger* disaster (Photos courtesy NASA)

U.S. FLAG HISTORICAL TIMELINE

1775 – The first American flag was the Grand Union flag. It consisted of thirteen alternating red and white stripes and the British Union Jack in the upper left-hand corner. It was first flown by the ships of the Colonial  Fleet on the Delaware River. It was also flown by John Paul Jones.

January 1, 1776 – George Washington orders that the Grand Union flag be flown above his base on Prospect Hill near Cambridge, Massachusetts. On that New Year's Day, the Continental Army was laying siege to Boston which had been taken over by the British Army.

May or June 1776 – This is when reports claim Betsy Ross sewed the first stars and stripes American flag, one month prior to the Declaration of Independence. These reports were made in 1870 (see attached paper, "The First American Flag and Who Made It" and accompanying affidavits). Many historians question whether she actually made the first stars and stripes. It is, however, generally acknowledged that she made flags for the Pennsylvania State Navy in 1777, and she continued to make American flags for fifty years.

One of her grandsons, William J. Canby, in 1870, in a paper he read before the meeting of the Historical Society of Pennsylvania, stated:

"It is not tradition, it is report from the lips of the principal participator in the transaction, directly told not to one or two, but a dozen or more living witnesses, of which I myself am one, though but a little boy when I heard it.... Colonel Ross with Robert Morris and General Washington, called on Mrs. Ross and told her they were a committee of Congress, and wanted her to make a flag from the drawing, a rough one, which, upon her suggestions, was redrawn by General Washington in pencil in her back parlor. This was prior to the Declaration of Independence. I fix the date to be during Washington's visit to Congress from New York in June, 1776, when he came to confer upon the affairs of the Army, the flag being no doubt, one of these affairs."

July 4, 1776 – The Declaration of Independence. The Grand Union Flag is our unofficial national flag.

June 14, 1777 – The Continental Congress first authorizes an official flag for the new nation. The resolution read: "Resolved: that the flag of the United States be thirteen stripes, alternate red and white; that the union be thirteen stars, white in a blue field, representing a new constellation."

The resolution gave no instruction as to how many points the stars should have, nor how the stars should be arranged on the blue union. Consequently, some flags had stars scattered on the blue field without any specific design, some arranged the stars in rows, and some in a circle. This practice continued until 1912 when the design of the flag was fixed by executive order.

There is no universally agreed-upon symbolism in the colors of the flag. One common interpretation is that the red symbolizes valor, zeal and fervency; the white symbolizes hope and purity; and the blue symbolizes reverence to God, loyalty, sincerity, justice and truth. The star is taken by many to symbolize dominion and sovereignty, as well as lofty aspirations. The constellation of the stars within the union, one star for each state, is considered to be emblematic of our federal constitution, which reserves to the states their individual sovereignty except as to the rights delegated to the federal government.

George Washington explained his interpretation of the symbolism of the flag as follows: "We take the stars from Heaven, the red from our mother country, separating it by white stripes, thus showing that we have separated from her, and the white stripes shall go down to posterity representing Liberty."

The thirteen stars and the thirteen stripes represented the first thirteen states: Delaware, Pennsylvania, New Jersey, Georgia, Connecticut, Massachusetts, Maryland, South Carolina, New Hampshire, Virginia, New York, North Carolina, and Rhode Island.

A tradition developed to fold the flag into a triangular shape, symbolizing the shape of the cocked hats worn by soldiers of the American Revolution.

The flag appears to have been designed by Francis Hopkinson, one of the signers of the Declaration of Independence who was also a lawyer, a poet, and an artist who then became a Congressman from New Jersey. He later attempted to be paid for his services, but his pay was blocked by his political opponents. Hopkinson's design had the stars arranged in staggered rows.

June 14 later came to be celebrated as "Flag Day."

August 3, 1777 – The new American flag is first flown from Fort Stanwix, on the site of the present city of Rome, New York.

August 6, 1777 – The new American flag first comes under fire in the Battle of Oriskany.

September 11, 1777 – The flag is first carried into battle at the Brandywine.

January 28, 1778 – The American flag first flies over foreign territory at Nassau, Bahama Islands. Fort Nassau was captured by the Americans in the course of the War for Independence.

1787 – Captain Robert Gray carries the flag around the world on his sailing vessel (around the tip of South America, to China, and beyond). He discovered a great river and named it after his boat, The Columbia. His discovery was the basis of America's claim to the Oregon Territory.

1790s – The "Betsy Ross flag" appears, which arranges the thirteen stars in a circle.

January 13, 1794 – Vermont had been admitted to the union in 1791 and Kentucky in 1792, making a total of 15 states. On this date in 1794, Congress adopts a resolution increasing the number of stars and stripes to 15 each.

May 1, 1795 – By the 1794 resolution, the 15-star, 15-stripe flag becomes official, and remains the official flag of the nation for twenty-three years.

June 1, 1795 – Tennessee is admitted to the Union as the 16th state, but the flag design remains the same.

March 1, 1803 – Ohio is admitted as the 17th state.

April 30, 1812 – Louisiana becomes the 18th state. We still have 15 stars and 15 stripes in the flag.

September 14, 1814 – During the British bombardment of Fort McHenry in the War of 1812, Francis Scott Key writes "The Star-Spangled Banner." The flag at the time has fifteen stars and fifteen stripes. The Star-Spangled Banner didn't officially become the national anthem until 1931.

The flag that flew over Ft. McHenry was made by Mary Young Pickersgill. Her home in Baltimore was later enshrined as the "Flag House." Situated on the corner of Albemarle and Pratt streets in Baltimore, it is preserved as a National Historic Landmark.

1816-1817 – Indiana and Mississippi are admitted to the union, bringing the number of states to 20.

December 10, 1817 – With the continual growth of the Union, President Monroe signs an act of Congress requiring that the flag of the United States have a union of twenty stars, white on a blue field, and that upon admission of each new State into the Union, one star be added to the union of the flag on the fourth of July following its date of admission. The number of stripes was reduced by this law to always be thirteen, representing the original thirteen states. This law went into effect on April 4, 1818, and is the current law in effect regulating the design of the flag. Again, it makes no specifications as to the dimensions of the flag or the arrangements of the stars, those details being left to flag manufacturers. There were some who continued to arrange the stars in a circle. Other variations in design occurred, and it was common during the Civil War for the stars and stripes to display gold stars.

In 1912 the design was finally fixed by executive order of President Taft. It was changed in 1959 upon the admission of more states by President Eisenhower.

The exact wording of the Flag Act is as follows: "That from and after the fourth day of July next, the flag of the United States be thirteen horizontal stripes, alternate red and white; that the union be twenty stars, white in a blue field. And be it further enacted, that on the admission of every state into the Union, one star be added to the union of the flag; and that such addition shall take effect on the fourth of July next succeeding such admission."

July 4, 1819 – With the admission of Illinois to the Union on December 3, 1818, the twenty-first star is automatically added to the flag, under the new law.

July 4, 1820 – Two stars added after the admission of Alabama and Maine.

1820 – First flag on Pikes Peak, Colorado

July 4, 1822 – Admission of Missouri brings the number of stars to 24.

August 10, 1831 – The name "Old Glory" is given to our flag by Captain William Driver of the brig Charles Doggett.

July 4, 1836 – Flag with 25 stars (Arkansas)

July 4, 1837 – Flag with 26 stars (Michigan)

July 4, 1845 – Flag with 27 stars (Florida)

July 4, 1846 – Flag with 28 stars (Texas)

July 4, 1847 – Flag with 29 stars (Iowa)

July 4, 1848 – Flag with 30 stars (Wisconsin)

July 4, 1851 – Flag with 31 stars (California)

July 4, 1858 – Flag with 32 stars (Minnesota)

July 4, 1859 – Flag with 33 stars (Oregon)

June 14, 1861 – The first Flag Day celebration occurs in Hartford, Connecticut, during the first summer of the Civil War. The flag continues to have 33 stars, even though the southern states have seceded from the Union.

July 4, 1861 – Flag with 34 stars; (Kansas). The first Confederate Flag (Stars and Bars) is adopted in Montgomery, Alabama.

June 20, 1863 – The 40 western counties of Virginia, not wanting to be separated from the Union with the rest of Virginia, had met and formed their own government. On this day, West Virginia was formally admitted into the Union as the 35th state.

July 4, 1863 – Flag with 35 stars (West Virginia)

July 4, 1865 – Flag with 36 stars (Nevada)

July 4, 1867 – Flag with 37 stars (Nebraska)

1869 – The American flag is printed on a postage stamp for the first time.

June 14, 1877 – The first national observance of Flag Day occurs on the 100th anniversary of the original flag resolution by the Continental Congress.

July 4, 1877 – Flag with 38 stars (Colorado)

July 4, 1890 – Flag with 43 stars (North Dakota, South Dakota, Montana, Washington, Idaho)

July 4, 1891 – Flag with 44 stars (Wyoming)

October 12, 1892 – The "Pledge of Allegiance" is first used in public schools to celebrate the 400th anniversary of the discovery of America. It was published in a magazine called *The Youth's Companion*, and written by Francis Bellamy. The original version pledged allegiance to "my flag." In 1923, the National Flag Conference changed that wording to "the flag of the United States of America." The words "under God" were added on June 14, 1954.

July 4, 1896 – Flag with 45 stars (Utah)

1890s – While Flag Day is still not an official celebration, its observance becomes more and more popular. Numerous patriotic societies and veterans groups become identified with the Flag Day movement. Schools, in particular, promote Flag Day as a means of "Americanizing" immigrant children and stimulating patriotism.

July 4, 1908 – Flag with 46 stars (Oklahoma)

1909 – Robert Peary places the flag his wife sewed atop the North Pole. He leaves pieces of another flag along the way. While the action was controversial, he was never censured for this.

June 24, 1912 – An executive order from President Taft finally uniformly establishes the proportions of the flag and fixes the pattern of stars. With the new states of New Mexico and Arizona being added to the union, it is decreed that the 48 stars would be in six horizontal rows of eight each, a single point of each star to be upward. Prior to this time, the proportions of the stripes and the positions of the stars were left to the flag manufacturers. This executive order establishes a precedent for fixing the design of the flag, and, when the 49th and 50th stars were added in 1959 and 1960, the arrangement of the stars is fixed again by executive order, this time from President Eisenhower.

July 4, 1912 – Flag with 48 stars (New Mexico, Arizona)

June 14, 1916 – Flag Day becomes an official national observance by virtue of a proclamation from President Woodrow Wilson.

1917 – The Valley Forge Flag Company begins making American flags.

March 3, 1931 – By act of Congress "The Star-Spangled Banner" becomes our national anthem.

February 23, 1945 – Photographer Joe Rosenthal snaps the famous photograph of United States Marines risking their lives to raise the American flag on Mount Suribachi on the Japanese island of Iwo Jima, four days after the beginning of the American invasion of that island. Fighting there continues for 31 more days, with heavy casualties, before the island finally falls to the Americans.

When the photograph is shown in the United States, it causes an immediate sensation. Members of the United States Senate call for the erection of a national monument modeled after the photograph.

August 14, 1945 – The tattered flag that flew over Pearl Harbor on December 7, 1941, is flown over the White House when the Japanese accept surrender terms.

September 28, 1945 – The American flag that flew on the Battleship *Missouri* during Japanese surrender ceremonies is hoisted at Pearl Harbor, Hawaii, in celebration of the American victory.

August 3, 1949 – Congress passes a law, and President Harry Truman signs it, permanently making June 14th to be Flag Day. However, it is not a legal holiday except in Pennsylvania.

June 14, 1954 – On Flag Day, 1954, The United States Congress adds the words "under God" to the Pledge of Allegiance. Of this action, President Dwight D. Eisenhower says, "In this way we are reaffirming the transcendence of religious faith in America's heritage and future; in this way we shall constantly strengthen those spiritual weapons which forever will be our country's most powerful resource in peace and war."

November 10, 1954 – The Iwo Jima memorial, formally known as the Marine Corps War Memorial, constructed by sculptor Felix DeWeldon, is dedicated by President Eisenhower in Arlington National Cemetery.

July 4, 1959 – Flag with 49 stars (Alaska)

July 4, 1960 – Flag with 50 stars (Hawaii)

1963 – The American flag is placed on top of Mount Everest by Barry Bishop.

1968 – The National Flag Foundation (NFF) is established in Pittsburg, Pennsylvania. NFF is America's leading non-profit patriotic educational organization promoting respect for the American flag.

July 20, 1969 – The American flag is posted on the moon in the *Sea of Tranquility* by *Apollo* astronauts Neil Armstrong and Edward "Buzz" Aldrin.

February 22, 1980 – Mike Eruzione scores 3 goals, including the winning goal, as the U.S. Hockey team beats the unbeatable Soviet team 4-3 in a stunning upset, in front of a boisterous, flag-waving crowd. Eruzione skates around the arena after the victory wrapped in an American flag. The Americans had been defeated by the Soviets 10-3 in an exhibition match only a week before the Olympics.

1984 – The *Challenger* flag is manufactured by the Valley Forge Flag Company.

January 25, 1985 – The *Challenger* flag flies briefly over the United States Capitol.

February 1985 – The *Challenger* flag is presented to its scout troop, Troop 514 of Monument, Colorado.

January 28, 1986 at 11:38 a.m. EST – The Space Shuttle *Challenger* lifts off its launch pad at the Kennedy Space Center, with an American flag from Troop 514 of Monument, Colorado, carried in the official flight kit.

January 28, 1986 at 11:40 a.m. EST – 70 seconds after launch, the *Challenger* Shuttle explodes, killing all seven crew members. The *Challenger* flag is lost among the wreckage.

December 18, 1986 – The *Challenger* flag is returned from the wreckage to Troop 514 by Eagle Scout/Astronaut/ Colonel Guy Bluford, at a special ceremony at Falcon Air Force Station, Colorado.

December 19, 1986 – The Challenger Flag is designated the official flag of the Bi-Centennial of the Constitution of the United States by Chief Justice of the Supreme Court, Warren Burger.

September 17, 1987 – BSA Troop 514 presents the *Challenger* Flag to 14,000 guests as part of the opening ceremony of the Bicentennial Gala Event.

September 18, 1987 – The *Challenger* Flag is flown again over the United States Capitol—completing an amazing journey from the Capitol, to a Boy Scout Troop in Colorado, to Johnson Space Center, to Kennedy Space Center, to the official flight kit of the Space Shuttle *Challenger*, to the edge of space, to the bottom of the Atlantic Ocean—and all the way back.

September 19, 1987 – BSA Troop 514 unfurls the *Challenger* Flag at the gravesite of the *Challenger* Astronauts in Arlington National Cemetery—honoring those who gave it flight.

April 20, 1988 – In a surprise ruling, the Texas court of criminal appeals, by a 5-4 vote, overturns the conviction of Gregory Lee Johnson. In 1984, Gregory Lee Johnson had joined a group of anti-Reagan protesters to oppose "the American exploitation of third world countries" by burning an American flag. He was convicted under Texas' venerated objects law. The appeals court rules that his conviction violated Johnson's first amendment right of freedom of expression.

June 21, 1989 – In a 5-4 decision, the United States Supreme Court rules in the case of Texas v. Johnson, and holds that burning or otherwise desecrating the American flag is protected free speech.

September 1989 – The United States Congress approves the Flag Protection Act of 1989. The vote in the House of Representatives was 380-38; in the Senate it was 91-9. President George H.W. Bush allows it to become law without his signature, saying that he believes that the legislation would require a constitutional amendment.

October 30, 1989 – The day the Flag Protection Act of 1989 takes effect, hundreds of protesters burn American Flags.

June 11, 1990 – In the cases of U.S. v Haggerty and U.S. v Eichman, the United States Supreme Court rules that the Flag Protection Act of 1989 is unconstitutional.

December 12, 1995 – The Flag Desecration Constitutional Amendment passes the House of Representatives by a vote of 312 to 120. In the Senate, however, the vote is 63-36, 3 votes short of the required 2/3 majority. This Amendment to the Constitution would have allowed Congress to make laws prohibiting flag burning or other activities that desecrate the flag. Supporters of this Amendment continue to labor for its passage.

September 11, 2001 – Hijacked commercial airliners destroy the twin towers of the World Trade Center and strike the Pentagon, killing thousands of people. Within minutes, the Valley Forge Flag Company is flooded with calls to buy American flags. While Americans purchase about 2 million house flags annually, on this one day an estimated 25 to 30 million people wanted flags right away.

February 8, 2002 – Eight athletes, escorted by New York City firefighters and Port Authority police, carry the tattered American flag that had been found in the rubble of the World Trade Center into the Olympic stadium at Salt Lake City before a reverent

(Photo courtesy American Forces Information Service)

crowd of 60,000 people. During the Olympics, the *Challenger* flag is on public display at the Joseph Smith Memorial Building in downtown Salt Lake City.

February 1, 2003 – The Space Shuttle *Columbia* disintegrates in flames over Texas, minutes prior to its scheduled landing after an otherwise successful 16-day mission. All seven astronauts aboard are killed.

THE FIRST AMERICAN FLAG AND WHO MADE IT

By William J. Canby, grandson of Elizabeth Claypoole (Betsy Ross).

An excerpt of a paper read before the Historical Society of Pennsylvania in 1870

According to a well sustained tradition in the family of Elizabeth Claypoole (then Elizabeth Ross) this lady is the one to whom belongs the honor of having made with her own hands the first flag. Three of her daughters are still living who confirm this statement, not from their own knowledge, for the flag was made before they were born, but from the recollection of their mother's often repeated narration and from hearing it told by others who were cognizant of the facts during their childhood; and there is also yet living a niece of Mrs. Claypoole's, Mrs. Margaret Boggs (now in her 95th year) who resides with a niece in Germantown, Philadelphia, and still has full possession of all her faculties, who remembers well the incidents of the transaction as she heard it told, in her intimate intercourse with the family many times.

The writer of this paper in the year 1857 had a conversation on the subject with the eldest daughter of

Elizabeth Claypoole, then in active life, but since deceased, Mrs. Clarissa S. Wilson, who succeeded her mother in the business of flag and color making and continued it for many years. Mrs. Wilson's statement was put in writing at the time, as have been also the statements of her sisters and of Mrs. Boggs and the substance of them is now given.

We believe the fact is not generally known that to Philadelphia belongs the honor of having first flung the "star-spangled banner" to the breeze, and that to a Philadelphia lady, long since gathered to her fathers, belongs the honor of having made the first flag with her own hands.

A little two story and attic house, with over-hanging eaves and pent-eaves, and a porch at the door, the brick front decorated with alternate glazed bricks, situated on the North side of Arch Street a few doors East of Third street, was the scene of the birth place of the star-spangled banner. (The house is now standing, the only one of a row that once occupied that part of the street. Its present number is 239; the old number was 89). This unpretending and humble abode was once distinguished with a tin sign upon the window containing the words Elizabeth Ross Upholsterer.

Within that window might be seen specimens of her craft in the shape of a few pillows, with now and then a piece of fine embroidery or other needle work; and, further in, was no doubt often visible through the panes, the pleasant and by no means unhandsome features of Elizabeth, or Betsy as she was familiarly called, and perhaps also the face of one or two young girls, her assistants.

Betsy drove a thriving trade, was notable, prudent and industrious, and never had any time to spend in street gaping or gossip, and was, consequently, very much respected by her neighbors. She was the daughter of an influential and respectable member of the Society of Friends, a House Carpenter by trade, whose name was

Samuel Griscom. He lived on the North side of Arch Street, opposite Friends burying ground (where the meeting house now stands) between Third and Fourth Streets, and had his shop on the rear of his lot upon Cherry Street. He had a numerous family, the seventh of whom was Elizabeth. She being unwilling to remain a dependent upon her father had accepted a situation as apprentice in a large upholstering establishment in this city where many hands were employed and had there learned her trade; and had captivated with her modest deportment a youth, John Ross, her fellow apprentice. (This John Ross was a son of the Rev. Aeneas Ross then residing at New Castle, Del. at one time assistant minister of Christ Church in Philadelphia). John and Betsy formed a partnership for life, were married, and, on his arriving at age, were established in business by his father; but the partnership was dissolved in two years by John's death, leaving Mrs. Ross, a young widow, without any children. Overcome with grief she allowed her establishment to be broken up by her relatives, and sold out at a considerable sacrifice, and she returned to her father's house to mourn her sad bereavement, and the early blighting of her hopes and plans for life. Here, however, she soon again became discontented with her dependent position and saw the mistake she had made in giving up her business.

Without any means to depend upon but her hands, she rented the little house we have described, and "hung up her shingle," inviting her former customers to her shop. With all her patient industry and perseverance, however, she found it difficult to get along, as the "hard times" brought about by the revolutionary war, came upon her. She often pondered over the future, and brooded sometimes almost to despondency upon her troubles, yet she always rallied when she reflected upon the goodness of Providence who had never deserted her.

Sitting sewing in her shop one day with her girls around her, several gentlemen entered. She recognized one of these as the uncle of her deceased husband, Col. GEORGE ROSS, a delegate from Pennsylvania to Congress. She also knew the handsome form and features of the dignified, yet graceful and polite Commander in Chief, who, while he was yet COLONEL WASHINGTON had visited her shop both professionally and socially many times, (a friendship caused by her connection with the Ross family). They announced themselves as a committee of congress, and stated that they had been appointed to prepare a flag, and asked her if she thought she could make one, to which she replied, with her usual modesty and self reliance, that "she did not know but she could try; she had never made one but if the pattern were shown to her she had not doubt of her ability to do it." The committee was shown into her back parlor, the room back of the shop, and Col. Ross produced a drawing, roughly made, of the proposed flag. It was defective to the clever eye of Mrs. Ross and unsymmetrical, and she offered suggestions which Washington and the committee readily approved.

What all these suggestions were we cannot definitely determine, but they were of sufficient importance to involve an alteration and re-drawing of the design, which was then and there done by General George Washington, in pencil, in her back parlor. One of the alterations had reference to the shape of the stars. In the drawing they were made with six points. Mrs. Ross at once said that this was wrong; the stars should be five pointed; they were aware of that, but thought there would be some difficulty in making a five pointed star. "Nothing easier" was her prompt reply and folding a piece of paper in the proper manner, with one clip of her ready scissors she quickly displayed to their astonished vision the five pointed star; which accordingly took its place in the national standard. General Washington was the active one in making the design, the others having little or nothing to do with it. When it was completed, it was given to William Barrett, painter, to paint.

He had no part in the design, he only did the painting. (He was a first rate artist. He lived in a large three story brick house on the East side of an alley which ran back to the Pennsylvania Academy for young ladies, which was kept by James A Neal; said to be the best institution of the kind at that time in Philadelphia. The house is yet standing.)

The committee suggested Mrs. Ross to call at a certain hour at the counting house of one of their number, a shipping merchant, on the wharf. Mrs. Ross was punctual to the appointment. The gentleman drew out of a chest an old ship's color, which he loaned her to show her how the sewing was done, and also the drawing painted by Barrett. Other designs had been prepared by the committee and one or two of them were placed in the hands of other seamstresses to be made. Betsy Ross went diligently to work upon her flag, carefully examining the peculiar stitch in the old ship's color, which had been given her as a specimen, and recognizing, with the eye of a good mechanic its important characteristics, strength and elasticity.

The flag was soon finished, and Betsy returned it, the first 'star-spangled banner' that ever floated upon the breeze, to her employer. It was run up to the peak of one of his ships lying at the wharf, and received the unanimous approval of the committee and of a little group of bystanders looking on, and the same day was carried into the State House and laid before Congress, with a report from the committee. The next day Col. Ross called upon Betsy, and informed her that her work had been approved and her flag adopted; and he now requested her to turn her whole attention to the manufacture of flags, and gave her an unlimited order for as many as she could make; desiring her to go out forthwith and buy all the "bunting and tack" in the city, and make flags as fast as possible. Here was astounding mews [sic] to Betsy! Her largest ideas of business heretofore had been confined to the furnishing of one or two houses at a time with beds, curtains and carpets; and she had only recently been depressed with the prospect of losing much of this limited business by reason of the high prices of materials, and the consequent retrenchment by citizens in luxuries that could be dispensed with. She sat ruminating upon her sudden good fortune some minutes before it occurred to her that she had not the means to make the extensive purchases required by the order; and, therefore, she would be utterly helpless to fill it; for these were the days of cash transactions, and such a thing as a poor person getting credit for a large amount of goods was altogether unheard of. Here was a dilemma. What was she to do? Like many others, she began already to doubt her good fortune and to dash her rising hopes with the reflections, "this is too good luck for me, it cannot be." Rising superior to this, however, she said to herself, "We are not creatures of luck: have I not found that the Good One has never deserted me, and He will not now. I will buy all the bunting I can, and make it into these flags, and will explain to Mr. Ross why I cannot get anymore. He will, no doubt, give orders to others, and so I shall lose a large part of this business: but I must be satisfied with a moderate share of it, and grateful too." So she went to work. Scarcely had she finished her cogitations when Col. Ross re-entered the shop. "It was very thoughtless of me," he remarked, "when I was just here now, that I did not offer to supply you with the means for making these purchases; it might inconvenience you," he said delicately, "to pay out so much cash at once, here is something to begin with" (giving her a one hundred pound note) "and you must draw on me at sight for what ever you require."

Mrs. Ross was now effectively set up in the business of flag and color making for the government; through all her after life, which was a long, useful and eventful one, she "never knew what it was," to use her own expression, "to want employment," this business (flag-making for the government) remaining with her and in her family for many years. She was afterwards twice married; once to Joseph Ashbourne, a shipmaster in the merchant services, by whom she had one daughter, named Eliza, and after his death, to John Claypoole.

AFFIDAVIT DATED MAY 27, 1870

Affidavit of Sophia B. Hildebrant, daughter of Clarissa S. Wilson and granddaughter of Elizabeth Claypoole (Betsy Ross).

"I remember to have heard my grandmother Elizabeth Claypoole frequently narrate the circumstance of her having made the first star-spangled banner; that it was a specimen flag made to the order of the committee of Congress, acting in conjunction with General Washington, who called upon her personally at her store in Arch Street, below Third Street, Philadelphia, shortly before the Declaration of Independence; that she said that General Washington made a redrawing of the design with his own hands after some suggestions made by her; and that this specimen flag was exhibited in Congress by the committee, with a report, and the flag and report were approved and adopted by the Congress; and she received an unlimited order from the committee to make flags for the government, and to my knowledge she continued to manufacture the government flags for about fifty years, when my mother succeeded her in the business, in which I assisted. I believe the facts stated in the foregoing article, entitled 'The First American Flag, and Who Made It,' are all strictly true."

Witness my hand at Philadelphia the Twenty-seventh day of May A.D. 1870.

Witnesses present.

Isaac R. Oakford

Charles H. Evans

S.B. Hildebrandt.

State of Pennsylvania,

City of Philadelphia SS

On the Twenty-seventh day of May A.D. 1870, Before me Charles H. Evans, a Notary Public in and for the Common-wealth of Pennsylvania, duly commissioned, residing in the said City of Philadelphia personally appeared the within named Sophia B. Hildebrandt, who being duly affirmed did depose and say that the statements within certified to by her are all strictly true, according to the best of her knowledge and belief, and that she is a daughter of Clarissa S. Wilson, who was a daughter of Elizabeth Claypoole.

Affirmed and subscribed before me, this day and year aforesaid.

Witness my hand and Notarial seal.

Charles H. Evans

S.B. Hildebrant

AFFIDAVIT DATED JUNE 3, 1870

Affidavit of Margaret Donaldson Boggs, daughter of Sarah Donaldson, who was a sister of Elizabeth Claypoole (Betsy Ross).

"I, Margaret Boggs, of the City of Philadelphia, Widow, do hereby certify that I have heard my aunt, Elizabeth Claypoole say many times, that she made the first star-spangled banner that ever was made with her own hands; that she made it on the order of General Washington and a committee of the Continental Congress, who together called personally upon her at her house on the North side Arch Street below Third Street, Philadelphia, some time previously to the Declaration of Independence. That they brought with them a drawing, roughly made, of the proposed flag; that she said it was wrong, and proposed alterations, which Washington and the Committee approved; that one of these alterations was in regard to the number of points of the star; that she said it should be five-pointed, and showed them how to fold a piece of paper in the proper manner, and with one cut of the scissors, to make a five-pointed star; that General Washington sat at a table in her back parlor, where they were, and made a drawing of the flag embodying her suggestions, and that she made the flag according to this drawing, and the committee carried it before Congress, by whom it was approved and adopted. That she then received orders to make flags for the government as fast as possible; and from that time forward, for upwards of fifty years she made all the flags made for the United States in Philadelphia, and largely for the other naval stations. I was for many years a member of her family, and aided her in the business. I believe the facts stated in the foregoing article entitled 'The First American Flag and Who Made It,' which has now been read to me are all strictly true."

Witness my hand at Germantown in the City of Philadelphia, this Third day of June A.D. 1870.

Witnesses present.
Charles B. Engle
Stephen T. Beale
Margaret Boggs
State of Pennsylvania
City of Philadelphia SS.

On the Third day of June A.D. 1870, before me Charles B. Engle a Notary Public in and for the Commonwealth of Pennsylvania, duly commissioned, residing in the said City of Philadelphia, personally appeared the within named Margaret Boggs, who being duly affirmed did depose and say that the statements within certified to by her are all strictly true, according to the best of her knowledge and belief, and that she is a daughter of Sarah Donaldson, who was a sister of Elizabeth Claypoole.

Affirmed and subscribed before me day and year aforesaid. Witness my hand and Notarial Seal

M. Boggs
Charles B. Engle, Notary Public.

AFFIDAVIT DATED JULY 31, 1871

Affidavit of Rachel Fletcher, a daughter of Elizabeth Claypoole (Betsy Ross)

"I remember having heard my mother Elizabeth Claypoole say frequently that she, with her own hands, (while she was the widow of John Ross,) made the first star-spangled banner that ever was made. I remember to have heard her also say that it was made on the order of a Committee, of whom Col. Ross was one, and that Robert Morris was also one of the Committee. That General Washington, acting in conference with the committee, called with them at her house. This house was on the North side of Arch Street a few doors below Third Street, above Bread Street, a two story house, with attic and a dormer window, now standing, the only one of the row left, the old number being 89; it was formerly occupied by Daniel Niles, Shoemaker. Mother at first lived in the house next East, and when the war came, she moved into the house of Daniel Niles. That it was in the month of June 1776, or shortly before the Declaration of Independence that the committee called on her. That the member of the committee named Ross was an uncle of her deceased husband. That she was previously well acquainted with Washington, and that he had often been in her house in friendly visits, as well as on business. That she had embroidered ruffles for his shirt bosoms and cuffs, and that it was partly owing to his friendship for her that she was chosen to make the flag. That when the committee (with General Washington) came into her store she showed them into her parlor, back of her store; and one of them asked her if she could make a flag and that she replied that she did not know but she could try. That they then showed her a drawing roughly executed, of the flag as it was proposed to be made by the committee, and that she saw in it some defects in its proportions and the arrangement and shape of the stars. That she said it was square and a flag should be one third longer than its width, that the stars were scattered promiscuously over the field, and she said they should be either in lines or in some adopted form as a circle, or a star, and that the stars were six-pointed in the drawing, and she said they should be five pointed. That the gentlemen of the committee and General Washington very respectfully considered the suggestions and acted upon them, General Washington seating himself at a table with a pencil and paper, altered the drawing and then made a new one according to the suggestions of my mother. That General Washington seemed to her to be the active one in making the design, the others having little or nothing to do with it. That the committee then requested her to call on one of their number, a shipping merchant on the wharf, and then adjourned. That she was punctual to her appointment, and then the gentleman drew out of a chest an old ship's color which he loaned her to show her how the sewing was done; and also gave her the drawing finished according to her suggestions. That this drawing was done in water colors by William Barrett, an artist, who lived on the North side of Cherry Street above Third Street, a large three story brick house on the West side of an alley which ran back to the Pennsylvania Academy for Young Ladies, kept by James A. Neal, the best school of the kind in the city at that time. That Barrett only did the painting, and had nothing to do with the design. He was often employed by mother afterwards to paint the coats of arms of the United States and of the States on silk flags. That other designs had also been made by the committee and given to other seamstresses to make, but that they were not approved. That mother went diligently to work upon her flag and soon finished it, and returned it, the first star-spangled banner that ever was made, to her employers, that it was run up to the peak of one of the vessels belonging to one of the committee then lying at the wharf, and was received with shouts of applause by the few bystanders who happened to be looking on. That the committee on the same day carried the flag into the Congress sitting in the State House, and made a report presenting the flag and the drawing and that Congress unanimously approved and accepted the report. That the next day Col. Ross called upon my mother and informed her that her work had been approved and her flag adopted, and he gave orders for the purchase of all the materials and the manufacture of as many flags as she could make. And that from that time forward, for over fifty years she continued to make flags for the United States Government."

"I believe the facts stated in the foregoing Article entitled 'The First American Flag and Who Made It,' are all strictly true. This affidavit having been signed by Rachel Fletcher with violet ink, the signature has faded, but is at this time, Seventh Month 24th, 1908, still plainly legible."

Rachel Fletcher

I, Mary Fletcher Wigert, daughter of the said Rachel Fletcher, recognize the signature in the rectangular space outlined in black above, as the signature of my mother Rachel Fletcher.

Mary Fletcher Wigert

Signed in the presence of Mary W. Miller Philadelphia Seventh Mo. 24th, 1908

State of New York

City of New York SS

On the 31st day of July A.D. 1871. Before me the subscriber a Notary Public in and for the Commonwealth of New York, duly commissioned, residing in the said City of New York, personally appeared the above named Rachel Fletcher, who being duly affirmed did depose and say that the statements above certified to by her are all strictly true according to the best of her knowledge and belief, and that she is a daughter of Elizabeth Claypoole. Affirmed and subscribed before me the day and year aforesaid. Witness my hand and Notarial Seal.

Th. J. McEvily

Notary Public City & Co. New York

CARING FOR, RESPECTING, AND HONORING YOUR FLAG

When Troop 514 of Monument Colorado landed in Philadelphia to prepare for the bicentennial celebrations, we learned that the Paul Harvey broadcast that morning ("The Rest of the Story") told the story of our Boy Scout Troop and the special flag which we carried. From the moment we landed, people noticing our uniforms would come up to us and ask, "Are you that Boy Scout Troop with the Flag from the *Challenger*?" When we responded that we were, they inevitably responded with a request to see and touch this great flag.

Our young men would proudly display their Flag and the people would respond in the very same way—every time. They would remove their hats if they were wearing one and then reach out and touch the Flag with tears running down their cheeks. It was the same in the airport, at our hotel, and on the streets of Philadelphia. Everywhere we went, people were honored to be in the presence of this great Flag and showered it with humble respect.

As we were standing outside of the Philadelphia center where the opening ceremonies would be held, a reporter came up to us and asked if we were the Troop in Paul Harvey's broadcast. When we confirmed that we were, he asked a few questions, then asked if he could take a photograph of the Flag for his newspaper. We said he could whereupon he reached out and took the flag into his hands. Then before any of us could react, he laid it on the ground, pointed his camera, and took a photo of it. We were stunned!

One of our young men immediately picked up the Flag and pressed it to his chest. The rest gave the reporter a verbal reprimand worthy of Betsy Ross or George Washington. After the reporter departed, the young men tearfully discussed whether they now had to burn the Flag. We discussed what had happened and the value of the Flag to others and resolved that we would never place our sacred charge into other hands until we knew that they would honor it and show it the respect that it deserved.

Most Americans love the emblem of their great nation. But not all of them understand how to properly treat the American Flag to preserve its honor. It is for this reason that our leaders have codified rules for the care and display of the American flag.

Those rules and guides can be found in the United States Code, Title 4, Flag and Seal, Seat of Government and the States, Chapter 1 - The Flag.

The US Code can also be found on the web at various sites, including the following: http://www4.law.cornell.edu/uscode. There are also many fine websites that provide additional graphics to guide you in proper display of your American flag.

Excerpts from the US Code are provided here so that each of you can know with a certainty how to properly care for, display, and honor your flags.

— William A. Tolbert

UNITED STATES CODE TITLE 4

FLAG AND SEAL, SEAT OF GOVERNMENT, AND THE STATES

CHAPTER 1 - THE FLAG*

Sec. 1. - Flag; stripes and stars on same

The flag of the United States shall be thirteen horizontal stripes, alternate red and white; and the union of the flag shall be forty-eight stars, white in a blue field.

Sec. 2. - Additional stars

On the admission of a new State into the Union one star shall be added to the union of the flag; and such addition shall take effect on the fourth day of July then next succeeding such admission.

Sec. 3. - Use of flag for advertising purposes; mutilation of flag

Any person who, within the District of Columbia, in any manner, for exhibition or display, shall place or cause to be placed any word, figure, mark, picture, design, drawing, or any advertisement of any nature upon any flag, standard, colors, or ensign of the United States of America; or shall expose or cause to be exposed to public view any such flag, standard, colors, or ensign upon which shall have been printed, painted, or otherwise placed, or to which shall be attached, appended, affixed, or annexed any word, figure, mark, picture, design, or drawing, or any advertisement of any nature; or who, within the District of Columbia, shall manufacture, sell, expose for sale, or to public view, or give away or have in possession for sale, or to be given away or for use for any purpose, any article or substance being an article of merchandise, or a receptacle for merchandise or article or thing for carrying or transporting merchandise, upon which shall have been printed, painted, attached, or otherwise placed a representation of any such flag, standard, colors, or ensign, to advertise, call attention to, decorate, mark, or distinguish the article or substance on which so placed shall be deemed guilty of a misdemeanor and shall be punished by a fine not exceeding $100 or by imprisonment for not more than thirty days, or both, in the discretion of the court. The words "flag, standard, colors, or ensign," as used herein, shall include any flag, standard, colors, ensign, or any picture or representation of either, or of any part or parts of either, made of any substance or represented on any substance, of any size evidently purporting to be either of said flag, standard, colors, or ensign of the United States of America or a picture or a representation of either, upon which shall be shown the colors, the stars and the stripes, in any number of either thereof, or of any part or parts of either, by which the average person seeing the same without deliberation may believe the same to represent the flag, colors, standard, or ensign of the United States of America.

Sec. 4. - Pledge of allegiance to the flag; manner of delivery

The Pledge of Allegiance to the Flag, "I pledge allegiance to the Flag of the United States of America, and to the Republic for which it stands, one Nation under God, indivisible, with liberty and justice for all," should be rendered by standing at attention facing the flag with the right hand over the heart. When not in uniform men should remove their headdress with their right hand and hold it at the left shoulder, the hand being over the heart. Persons in uniform should remain silent, face the flag, and render the military salute.

Sec. 5. - Display and use of flag by civilians; codification of rules and customs; definition

The following codification of existing rules and customs pertaining to the display and use of the flag of the United

States of America is established for the use of such civilians or civilian groups or organizations as may not be required to conform with regulations promulgated by one or more executive departments of the Government of the United States. The flag of the United States for the purpose of this chapter shall be defined according to sections 1 and 2 of this title and Executive Order 10834 issued pursuant thereto.

Sec. 6. - Time and occasions for display

(a) It is the universal custom to display the flag only from sunrise to sunset on buildings and on stationary flagstaffs in the open. However, when a patriotic effect is desired, the flag may be displayed 24 hours a day if properly illuminated during the hours of darkness.

(b) The flag should be hoisted briskly and lowered ceremoniously.

(c) The flag should not be displayed on days when the weather is inclement, except when an all weather flag is displayed.

(d) The flag should be displayed on all days, especially on New Year's Day, January 1; Inauguration Day, January 20; Martin Luther King Jr.'s birthday, third Monday in January; Lincoln's Birthday, February 12; Washington's Birthday, third Monday in February; Easter Sunday (variable); Mother's Day, second Sunday in May; Armed Forces Day, third Saturday in May; Memorial Day (half-staff until noon), the last Monday in May; Flag Day, June 14; Independence Day, July 4; Labor Day, first Monday in September; Constitution Day, September 17; Columbus Day, second Monday in October; Navy Day, October 27; Veterans Day, November 11; Thanksgiving Day, fourth Thursday in November; Christmas Day, December 25; and such other days as may be proclaimed by the President of the United States; the birthdays of States (date of admission); and on State holidays.

(e) The flag should be displayed daily on or near the

main administration building of every public institution.

(f) The flag should be displayed in or near every polling place on election days.

(g) The flag should be displayed during school days in or near every schoolhouse.

Sec. 7. - Position and manner of display

The flag, when carried in a procession with another flag or flags, should be either on the marching right; that is, the flag's own right, or, if there is a line of other flags, in front of the center of that line.

(a) The flag should not be displayed on a float in a parade except from a staff, or as provided in subsection (i) of this section.

(b) The flag should not be draped over the hood, top, sides, or back of a vehicle or of a railroad train or a boat. When the flag is displayed on a motorcar, the staff shall be fixed firmly to the chassis or clamped to the right fender.

(c) No other flag or pennant should be placed above or, if on the same level, to the right of the flag of the United States of America, except during church services conducted by naval chaplains at sea, when the church pennant may be flown above the flag during church services for the personnel of the Navy. No person shall display the flag of the United Nations or any other national or international flag equal, above, or in a position of superior prominence or honor to, or in place of, the flag of the United States at any place within the United States or any Territory or possession thereof: Provided, That nothing in this section shall make unlawful the continuance of the practice heretofore followed of displaying the flag of the United Nations in a position of superior prominence or honor, and other national flags in positions of equal prominence or honor, with that of the flag of the United States at the headquarters of the United Nations.

(d) The flag of the United States of America, when it is

displayed with another flag against a wall from crossed staffs, should be on the right, the flag's own right, and its staff should be in front of the staff of the other flag.

(e) The flag of the United States of America should be at the center and at the highest point of the group when a number of flags of States or localities or pennants of societies are grouped and displayed from staffs.

(f) When flags of States, cities, or localities, or pennants of societies are flown on the same halyard with the flag of the United States, the latter should always be at the peak. When the flags are flown from adjacent staffs, the flag of the United States should be hoisted first and lowered last. No such flag or pennant may be placed above the flag of the United States or to the United States flag's right.

(g) When flags of two or more nations are displayed, they are to be flown from separate staffs of the same height. The flags should be of approximately equal size. International usage forbids the display of the flag of one nation above that of another nation in time of peace.

(h) When the flag of the United States is displayed from a staff projecting horizontally or at an angle from the window sill, balcony, or front of a building, the union of the flag should be placed at the peak of the staff unless the flag is at half-staff. When the flag is suspended over a sidewalk from a rope extending from a house to a pole at the edge of the sidewalk, the flag should be hoisted out, union first, from the building.

(i) When displayed either horizontally or vertically against a wall, the union should be uppermost and to the flag's own right, that is, to the observer's left. When displayed in a window, the flag should be displayed in the same way, with the union or blue field to the left of the observer in the street.

(j) When the flag is displayed over the middle of the street, it should be suspended vertically with the union to the north in an east and west street or to the east in a north and south street.

(k) When used on a speaker's platform, the flag, if displayed flat, should be displayed above and behind the speaker. When displayed from a staff in a church or public auditorium, the flag of the United States of America should hold the position of superior prominence, in advance of the audience, and in the position of honor at the clergyman's or speaker's right as he faces the audience. Any other flag so displayed should be placed on the left of the clergyman or speaker or to the right of the audience.

(l) The flag should form a distinctive feature of the ceremony of unveiling a statue or monument, but it should never be used as the covering for the statue or monument.

(m) The flag, when flown at half-staff, should be first hoisted to the peak for an instant and then lowered to the half-staff position. The flag should be again raised to the peak before it is lowered for the day. On Memorial Day the flag should be displayed at half-staff until noon only, then raised to the top of the staff. By order of the President, the flag shall be flown at half-staff upon the death of principal figures of the United States Government and the Governor of a State, territory, or possession, as a mark of respect to their memory. In the event of the death of other officials or foreign dignitaries, the flag is to be displayed at half-staff according to Presidential instructions or orders, or in accordance with recognized customs or practices not inconsistent with law. In the event of the death of a present or former official of the government of any State, territory, or possession of the United States, the Governor of that State, territory, or possession may proclaim that the National flag shall be flown at half-staff. The flag shall be flown at half-staff 30 days from the death of the President or a former President; 10 days from the day of death of the Vice President, the Chief Justice or a retired Chief Justice of the United States, or the Speaker of the House of Representatives; from the day of death until interment of an Associate Justice of the Supreme Court, a Secretary of an executive or military department, a former Vice President, or the Governor of a State, territory, or possession; and on the day of death and the following day for a Member of Congress. The flag shall be flown at half-staff on Peace Officers Memorial Day, unless that day is also Armed Forces Day.

As used in this subsection -

(1) the term "half-staff" means the position of the flag when it is one-half the distance between the top and bottom of the staff;

(2) the term "executive or military department" means any agency listed under sections 101 and 102 of title 5, United States Code; and

(3) the term "Member of Congress" means a Senator, a Representative, a Delegate, or the Resident Commissioner from Puerto Rico.

(n) When the flag is used to cover a casket, it should be so placed that the union is at the head and over the left shoulder. The flag should not be lowered into the grave or allowed to touch the ground.

(o) When the flag is suspended across a corridor or lobby in a building with only one main entrance, it should be suspended vertically with the union of the flag to the observer's left upon entering. If the building has more than one main entrance, the flag should be suspended vertically near the center of the corridor or lobby with the union to the north, when entrances are to the east and west or to the east when entrances are to the north and south. If there are entrances in more than two directions, the union should be to the east

Sec. 8. - Respect for flag

No disrespect should be shown to the flag of the United

States of America; the flag should not be dipped to any person or thing. Regimental colors, State flags, and organization or institutional flags are to be dipped as a mark of honor.

(a) The flag should never be displayed with the union down, except as a signal of dire distress in instances of extreme danger to life or property.

(b) The flag should never touch anything beneath it, such as the ground, the floor, water, or merchandise.

(c) The flag should never be carried flat or horizontally, but always aloft and free.

(d) The flag should never be used as wearing apparel, bedding, or drapery. It should never be festooned, drawn back, nor up, in folds, but always allowed to fall free. Bunting of blue, white, and red, always arranged with the blue above, the white in the middle, and the red below, should be used for covering a speaker's desk, draping the front of the platform, and for decoration in general.

(e) The flag should never be fastened, displayed, used, or stored in such a manner as to permit it to be easily torn, soiled, or damaged in any way.

(f) The flag should never be used as a covering for a ceiling.

(g) The flag should never have placed upon it, nor on any part of it, nor attached to it any mark, insignia, letter, word, figure, design, picture, or drawing of any nature.

(h) The flag should never be used as a receptacle for receiving, holding, carrying, or delivering anything.

(i) The flag should never be used for advertising purposes in any manner whatsoever. It should not be embroidered on such articles as cushions or handkerchiefs and the like, printed or otherwise impressed on paper napkins or boxes or anything that is designed for temporary use and discard. Advertising signs should not be fastened to a staff or halyard from which the flag is flown.

(j) No part of the flag should ever be used as a costume or athletic uniform. However, a flag patch may be affixed to the uniform of military personnel, firemen, policemen, and members of patriotic organizations. The flag represents a living country and is itself considered a living thing. Therefore, the lapel flag pin being a replica, should be worn on the left lapel near the heart.

(k) The flag, when it is in such condition that it is no longer a fitting emblem for display, should be destroyed in a dignified way, preferably by burning.

Sec. 9. - Conduct during hoisting, lowering or passing of flag

During the ceremony of hoisting or lowering the flag or when the flag is passing in a parade or in review, all persons present except those in uniform should face the flag and stand at attention with the right hand over the heart. Those present in uniform should render the military salute. When not in uniform, men should remove their headdress with their right hand and hold it at the left shoulder, the hand being over the heart. Aliens should stand at attention. The salute to the flag in a moving column should be rendered at the moment the flag passes.

Sec. 10. - Modification of rules and customs by President

Any rule or custom pertaining to the display of the flag of the United States of America, set forth herein, may be altered, modified, or repealed, or additional rules with respect thereto may be prescribed, by the Commander in Chief of the Armed Forces of the United States, whenever he deems it to be appropriate or desirable; and any such alteration or additional rule shall be set forth in a proclamation.

*The flag of the United States for the purposes of this chapter shall be defined according to sections 1 and 2 of Title 4 and Executive Order 10834 issued pursuant thereto.

TITLE 36, CHAPTER 1
PATRIOTIC AND NATIONAL OBSERVANCES

Sec. 144. *Patriot* Day

(a) Designation. - September 11 is *Patriot* Day.

(b) Proclamation. - The President is requested to issue each year a proclamation calling on -

(1) State and local governments and the people of the United States to observe *Patriot* Day with appropriate programs and activities;

(2) all departments, agencies, and instrumentalities of the United States and interested organizations and individuals to display the flag of the United States at halfstaff on *Patriot* Day in honor of the individuals who lost their lives as a result of the terrorist attacks against the United States that occurred on September 11, 2001; and

(3) the people of the United States to observe a moment of silence on *Patriot* Day in honor of the individuals who lost their lives as a result of the terrorist attacks against the United States that occurred on September 11, 2001.

TITLE 36, CHAPTER 10
PATRIOTIC CUSTOMS

Sec. 171. National anthem; Star-Spangled Banner, conduct during playing

During rendition of the national anthem when the flag is displayed, all present except those in uniform should stand at attention facing the flag with the right hand over the heart. Men not in uniform should remove their headdress with their right hand and hold it at the left shoulder, the hand being over the heart. Persons in uniform should render the military salute at the first note of the anthem and retain this position until the last note. When the flag is not displayed, those present should face toward the music and act in the same manner they would if the flag were displayed there.

Sec. 172. Pledge of Allegiance to the flag; manner of delivery

The Pledge of Allegiance to the Flag, "I pledge allegiance to the Flag of the United States of America, and to the Republic for which it stands, one Nation under God, indivisible, with liberty and justice for all," should be rendered by standing at attention facing the flag with the right hand over the heart. When not in uniform men should remove their headdress with their right hand and hold it at the left shoulder, the hand being over the heart. Persons in uniform should remain silent, face the flag, and render the military salute.

Sec. 173. Display and Use of flag by civilians; codification of rules and customs; definition

The following codification of existing rules and customs pertaining to the display and use of the flag of the United States of America is established for the use of such civilians or civilian groups or organizations as may not be required to conform with regulations promulgated by one or more executive departments of the Government of the United States. The flag of the United States for the purpose of this chapter shall be defined according to Title 4, United States Code, chapter 1, section 1 and section 2 and Executive Order 10834 issued pursuant thereto.

Sec. 174. Time and occasions for display

(a) It is the universal custom to display the flag only from sunrise to sunset on buildings and on stationary flagstaffs in the open. However, when a patriotic effect is desired, the flag may be displayed twenty-four hours a day if properly illuminated during the hours of darkness.

(b) The flag should be hoisted briskly and lowered ceremoniously.

(c) The flag should not be displayed on days when the weather is inclement, except when an all weather flag is displayed.

(d) The flag should be displayed on all days, especially on New Year's Day, January 1;

Inauguration Day, January 20;

Lincoln's Birthday, February 12;

Washington's Birthday, third Monday in February;

Easter Sunday (variable);

Mother's Day, second Sunday in May;

Armed Forces Day, third Saturday in May:

Memorial Day (half-staff until noon), the last Monday in May;

Flag Day, June 14;

Independence Day, July 4;

Labor Day, first Monday in September;

Constitution Day, September 17;

Columbus Day, second Monday in October;

Navy Day, October 27;

Veterans Day, November 11;

Thanksgiving Day, fourth Thursday in November;

Christmas Day, December 25;

and such other days as may be proclaimed by the President of the United States; the birthdays of States (date of admission); and on State holidays.

(e) The flag should be displayed daily on or near the main administration building of every public institution.

(f) The flag should be displayed in or near every polling place on election days.

(g) The flag should be displayed during school days in or near every schoolhouse.

FLAG PRESENTATION

Presentation of the flag during a ceremony should be preceded by a brief talk emphasizing the importance of the occasion. Following the presentation all present should salute the flag, recite the pledge of allegiance, and sing the national anthem.

FOLDING THE FLAG

1. Two persons, facing each other, hold the flag waist high and horizontally between them.
2. The lower striped section is folded, lengthwise, over the blue field. Hold bottom to top and edges together securely.
3. Fold the flag again, lengthwise, folded edge to open edge.
4. A triangular fold is started along the length of the flag, from the end to the heading by bringing the striped corner of the folded edge to meet the open edge.
5. The outer point is turned inward parallel with the open edge, forming a second triangle.
6. Repeat the triangular folding until the entire length of the flag is folded.
7. When the flag is completely folded only the triangular blue field should be visible.

WASHING AND RETIRING FLAGS

The life of your flag depends on your care. Dirt can cut fabrics, dull colors, and cause wear. Most outdoor flags can be washed in mild detergent and thoroughly rinsed. Indoor and parade flags should be dry-cleaned. Many dry cleaners offer free cleaning of U.S. flags during the months of June and July. Damaged flags can be repaired and utilized as long as the overall dimensions are not noticeably altered. American Legion Posts and local governments often have facilities to dispose of unserviceable flags. Store your flags in a well ventilated area away from any harsh chemicals or cleaning compounds. If your flag gets wet, never store it until it is completely dry. Wet folds cause permanent creases. Dampness ruins fabric and causes mildew. Pole care is also related to flag care. Rust and scale cause permanent stains and some metallic oxides actually eat holes in fabric.

SIZES OF FLAGS

The size of the flag is determined by the exposed height of the flagpole from which it is flying. The only consideration is for the flag to be in proper proportion to its pole. Flags which fly from angled poles on homes and those which are displayed on standing poles in offices and other indoor displays are usually either 3' x 5' or 4' x 6'. Color guards usually carry flags measuring 4' x 6'. Other recommended sizes are shown in the following table:

Flagpole Height (ft.)	Flag Size (ft.)
20	4 x 6
25	5 x 8
40	6 x 10
50	8 x 12
60	10 x 15
70	12 x 18
90	15 x 25
125	20 x 30
200	30 x 40
250	40 x 50

THE FLAG TODAY

The flag of the United States of America has 13 horizontal stripes—7 red and 6 white—the red and white stripes alternating and a union which consists of white stars of 5 points on a blue field placed in the upper quarter next to the staff and extending to the lower edge of the fourth red stripe from the top. The number of stars equals the number of States in the Union. The proportions of the flag as prescribed by Executive Order of President Eisenhower on August 21, 1959, are as follows:

Hoist (width) of flag..................1.0
Fly (length) of flag.....................1.9
Hoist (width) of union...............0.5385
Fly (length) of union..................0.76
Width of each stripe.................0.0769
Diameter of each star..............0.0616

FLAG ANATOMY

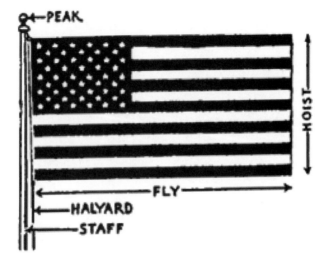

FLAGS AT THE UNITED STATES CAPITOL

No record has been found for the earliest date the flag was flown over the east and west fronts of the Capitol. Early engravings and lithographs in the office of the Architect of the Capitol show flags flying on either side of the original low dome above the corridors connecting the areas now known as Statuary Hall and the Old Senate Chamber.

After the addition of the new House and Senate wings in the 1850s, even before the great dome was completed in 1863, photographs of the period show flags flying over each new wing and the central east and west fronts.

The custom of flying the flags 24 hours a day over the east and west fronts was begun during World War I. This was done in response to requests received from all over the country urging that the flag of the United States be flown continuously over the public buildings in Washington, DC.

The east and west front flags, which are 8 x 12 feet, are replaced by new ones when they become worn and unfit for further use. Prior to machine-made flags, individuals were hired by the Congress to hand sew these flags.

HOW TO OBTAIN A FLAG FLOWN OVER THE CAPITOL

Constituents may arrange to purchase flags that have been flown over the Capitol by getting in touch with one of their Senators or their Representative. Requests can also be made to have a flag flown over the Capitol on a specific future date. A certificate signed by the Architect of the Capitol accompanies each flag. Flags now are available for purchase in sizes of 3' x 5' or 5' x 8' in fabrics of cotton and nylon.

INDEX

Novels by Gordon Ryan:

A Question of Consequence

Matthew Sterling discovers a Revolutionary War manuscript about the life of his sixth-great grandfather, Major Andrew McBride, that uncloaks a true patriot—and reveals the misguided citizens that pilloried him as a traitor. Soon, this Assistant City Manager of Snowy Ridge, Utah, finds himself embroiled in his own troubles. In the tumultuous aftermath of a local election gone awry, he has to decide whether or not to look the other way as unscrupulous politicians and bureaucrats seek to protect their schemes from public scrutiny. At stake is his reputation, his career, and his relationship with a beautiful Ph.D. genetic biology candidate. As he contemplates his choices, he wonders if he is destined to travel the same bitter path as his ancestor. $13.95, softcover.

State of Rebellion

A political suspense story about families and institutions caught up in a riptide of national intrigue, *State of Rebellion* is a patriotic story of contemporary politics, shattered family values, and the potential secession of California, depicting a nation torn by divided loyalties and far removed from the original intentions of America's Founding Fathers. $25.95, hardcover.

Easy Order From
CHECK YOUR LEADING BOOKSTORE
OR ORDER HERE

Item	Quantity	Price

Please include $1 shipping for each order.
Colorado residents add 7% sales tax.

___ My check or money order for $_____ is enclosed.
___ Please charge my credit card.

Name _____

Organization_____

Address_____

City/State/Zip_____

Phone_____ E-mail_____

___ MasterCard ___ Visa ___ Discover

Card #_____

Exp. Date_____

Signature_____

Please make your check payable and return to:
Mapletree Publishing Company
6233 Harvard Lane
Highlands Ranch, CO 80130

Call your credit card order to: 800-537-0414
Fax: 303-791-9028
Secure online ordering: www.mapletreepublishing.com